The JOY of FELLOWSHIP

J. Dwight Pentecost
Col. 1:18b

The JOY of FELLOWSHIP

A Study of First John

J. DWIGHT PENTECOST

Lamplighter Books Grand Rapids, Michigan
Zondervan Publishing House

The Joy of Fellowship: A Study of First John
Copyright © 1977 by J. Dwight Pentecost
All rights reserved

Lamplighter Books are published by the Zondervan Publishing House
1415 Lake Drive, S.E., Grand Rapids, Michigan 49506

Library of Congress Cataloging-in-Publication Data

Pentecost, J Dwight.
   The joy of fellowship
     p. cm.
   1. Bible. N.T. I John—Criticism, interpretation, etc.
I. Title.
  BS2805.2.P46   227'.94'06   77–13615
  ISBN 0-310-30921-2

                                                  CIP

Printed in the United States of America

90 91 92 93 94 / CH / 11 10 9 8 7

Contents

PREFACE

FELLOWSHIP IS ONE OF GOD'S greatest gifts; the believer delights to be in intimate relationship with fellow Christians. At the same time he longs to enter into an increasingly intimate relationship with the Father and the Savior. We were created with a need for fellowship, and we are restless and insecure until this becomes our living experience.

While there is much discussion about fellowship, little is understood of the bases, prerequisites, fruits, and the responsibilities of fellowship. John develops these truths in his first epistle; he wanted his spiritual children to enter into that life of intimate fellowship with the Father and Son that he had seen the Son live with His Father and into which the apostle himself had entered. It is our desire to enable you to enjoy that same life of fellowship.

These studies have grown out of lectures given to the students at Dallas Theological Seminary and to the Grace Bible Church family in Dallas where the author has served as pastor. They are put in this form to share the truths of First John with saints who hunger both for a more intimate fellowship with the Father and the Son and for increasing fellowship with the saints as well. May the Lord use these studies to that end.

1

A NEW KIND OF LIFE

1 John 1:1–2

To a nation staggering under the burden of the Mosaic law, Jesus announced that He had come to bring men abundant life. "I have come that they might have life, and that they might have it more abundantly" (John 10:10). He had come to share His life of oneness with the Father. Jesus used the illustration of a vine and a branch to teach this to His disciples (John 15). A branch is completely dependent on the root for life and is sustained only by sharing in the life of the root; fruit is only the life of the root manifested on the branch. Jesus was teaching that He is the source of life and that as men share His life they know the abundant life.

John, the son of Zebedee, heard Jesus speak of abundant life. This young man was in partnership with his father and brother in a lucrative fishing business. Jesus appeared on the shores of Galilee and "saw other two brethren, James the son of Zebedee, and John his brother, in a ship with Zebedee their father, mending their nets; and he called them. And they immediately left the ship and their father, and followed him" (Matt. 4:21–22). When John heard the Lord's summons he responded immediately and became a disciple, one of those who "believed on him" (John 2:11). Shortly after this John attended a wedding feast where he saw Jesus transform water into wine (John 2:11).

When Jesus singled out twelve men from among the many disciples following Him, John was among them (Luke 6). Jesus called them apostles or ''sent ones.'' John, who had left his fishing business, is now sent out to reach men and to draw them to the Lord Jesus.

The Lord took John, together with Peter and James, ''and went up into a mountain to pray. And as he prayed, the fashion of his countenance was altered, and his raiment was white and glistering'' (Luke 9:28–29). John stood on the Mount of Transfiguration and saw the glory that belonged to the Lord Jesus from all eternity, a glory veiled by His flesh.

John sat at the Passover feast at which Jesus instituted the Lord's Supper. ''Now there was leaning on Jesus' bosom one of his disciples, whom Jesus loved. Simon Peter therefore beckoned to him, that he should ask who it should be of whom he spake. He then lying on Jesus' breast saith unto him, Lord, who is it?'' (John 13:23–25).

At the Passover feast it was the custom of the Jews to recline on the left elbow on couches or pallets around a low table. So the one leaning on Jesus' bosom was at Jesus' right hand. The right hand was a place of honor, and so it was John who was appointed to a place of honor at the last Passover.

Jesus left the upper room and went to Gethsemane. ''They came to a place which was named Gethsemane: and he saith to his disciples, Sit ye here, while I shall pray. And he taketh with him Peter and James and John, and began to be sore amazed, and to be very heavy; and saith unto them, My soul is exceeding sorrowful unto death: tarry ye here, and watch'' (Mark 14:32–33). John was in the shadows of the Garden when Jesus poured out His prayer to the Father, ''If it be possible, let this cup pass from me: nevertheless not as I will, but as thou wilt'' (Matt. 26:39).

When Jesus went to Calvary, all the apostles forsook Him, save one. On the cross He saw His mother and the disciple He loved, and ''he saith unto his mother, Woman behold thy son! Then saith he to the disciple, Behold thy mother! And from that hour that disciple took her unto his own home" (John 19:26–27).

John was the first of the apostles to visit the empty tomb. The women who went to anoint Jesus' body saw the open grave and ran to tell the apostles.

> [Mary Magdalene] cometh to Simon Peter, and to the other disciple, whom Jesus loved [John], and saith unto them, They have taken away the Lord out of the sepulchre, and we know not where they have laid him. Peter therefore went forth, and that other disciple, and came to the sepulchre. So they ran both together: and the other disciple did outrun Peter, and came first to the sepulchre. And he stooping down, and looking in, saw the linen clothes lying . . . (John 20:2–5).

John was intimately associated with the Lord Jesus Christ from the outset of His ministry until He rose from the dead. No other apostle shared so much of the heart of Jesus.

According to church tradition, John became shepherd of the flock in Ephesus. Now the aged apostle writes an epistle to his spiritual children to share what he had seen and heard of the abundant life.

The Ephesian church had a stormy history. In Acts 19 its origin is traced to the apostle Paul leaving a fruitful ministry in Greece and coming to Ephesus, in the western portion of the Roman province of Asia, or Asia Minor. Ephesus was the social, economic, religious, cultural, and political center of that region.

Paul discovered some disciples of John the Baptist in Ephesus, people who believed John's promise that the Messiah was coming and were waiting for Him. No one had told them that the Messiah had already given His life as the Lamb of God, a sacrifice for the sins of the world. Paul singled out these disciples and opened up the Scriptures, explaining salvation through Christ, and with joy they embraced the Lord and entered into the body of Christ.

In the will and the wisdom of God Paul settled in Ephesus for two years and carried on perhaps his most fruitful ministry there. We would conclude from his epistle to the Ephesians that Ephesus was the strongest church that Paul established. But Paul knew from experience that whenever he moved on to new people and new areas and left a church behind, the enemies of the cross of Christ would flood in and Satan would use false apostles to deceive these babes in Christ and divert them from the truth. So Paul warned the elders:

> Take heed therefore unto yourselves, and to all the flock, over the which the Holy Ghost hath made you overseers, to feed the church of God, which he hath purchased with his own blood. For I know this, that after my departing shall grievous wolves enter in among you, not sparing the flock. Also of your own selves shall men arise, speaking perverse things, to draw away disciples after them (Acts 20:28–30).

Although the church had been forewarned, we learn from Paul's first epistle to Timothy that they did move in, perverting the thinking of the saints and dissuading the believers from following the true doctrine Paul had presented to them. These believers were brought under the crushing load of legalism and into bondage to the traditions of men. As a result they lost the liberty that belongs to the children of God. How Paul must have grieved!

When he wrote to the Philippians Paul promised to visit them after his release from prison. Paul honored that commitment, but he wrote to Timothy, "I besought thee to abide still at Ephesus, when I went into Macedonia, that thou mightest charge some that they teach no other doctrine, neither give heed to fables and endless genealogies, which minister questions, rather than godly edifying which is in faith" (1 Tim. 1:3–4). So Paul charged Timothy to correct false teaching and expel the false teachers. He wrote two epistles to Timothy to encourage him in this work of bringing these believers back into the glorious liberty that belonged to the sons of God. We learn how effective Timothy was from the Book of Revelation. Writing to the seven churches, John says to Ephesus, "I know thy works, and thy labour, and thy patience, and how thou canst not bear them which are evil; and thou hast tried them which say they are apostles, and are not, and has found them liars: And thou hast borne, and hast patience, and for my name's sake hast laboured, and hast not fainted" (Rev. 2:2–3). John can commend them because they have been brought back from the crippling legalism superimposed on them by false apostles and they had rid the church of the doctrine and the teachers.

John's first epistle begins, "That which was from the beginning, which we have heard, which we have seen with our eyes, which we have looked upon, and our hands have handled, of the Word of life" (v. 1). Many read this verse as though it says "The One who was from the beginning. . . ." But this epistle was not written to present the person of Christ; John had already done that in his Gospel.

John's Gospel begins, "In the beginning was the Word, and the Word was with God, and the Word was God. The same was in the beginning with God" (John 1:1–2). John affirms Christ's deity, eternalness, and His distinctness as a Person in the Trinity. John introduces Him as Creator and Revealer, for all things were made by Him and He is the Light of the world. Then, under the inspiration of the Holy Spirit, John presents a number of Christ's miracles to establish that He is the eternal Son of God. John presents the facts clearly and forcefully so that men may believe on Him.

Now, in his epistle, John shares truths concerning abundant life in Christ. So verse 1 should be understood this way: "That unique kind of life which was from the beginning, which we have heard, which we have seen, which we have looked upon, and our hands have handled, declare we unto you." A new kind of life available to men!

John is not presenting his testimony about the abundant life. He is providing the best evidence available, for Christ had taught and demonstrated the abundant life. So John shares what Christ shared with him while on earth.

First, he shares "that which we have heard." The Lord Jesus Christ revealed the Father with words. He spoke to the disciples about the Father and about His relationship to the Father.

Jesus also translated words into deeds. So John saw the abundant life of God reproduced in Jesus Christ—"which we have seen with our eyes."

Thirdly, John shares what "we have looked upon." "Looked upon" means "to give attention to," "to reflect on," so as to assimilate mentally. John had come to understand the meaning of the abundant life through his long and intimate association with Christ. John did not fully understand what Christ meant when He first spoke about sharing His life with men, but as he lived with Christ and saw His relationship to the Father, the Spirit illuminated his mind so that he understood Christ's pronouncement, "I have come that they might have life, and that they might have it more abundantly" (John 10:10).

Finally, the apostle addresses what "our hands have handled." When he refers to the hands, he implies appropriating or making something one's own. What Christ taught and lived John made his own, with the result that he possessed the abundant life.

John's writings emphasize several truths. First, Jesus claimed to be holy. He offered Himself as God come in the flesh. Surrounded by His enemies, Christ challenged them, "Which of you convinceth [convicts] me of sin?" (John 8:46). If one of them had been able to point to a single infraction of the Mosaic law, they would have silenced Him forever, but He was sinless and so His enemies stole away. In chapters one and two of his epistle John writes about Christ's life, and he reminds us that God is light, that is, absolute holiness, and he shows the demands that this holiness makes on one who would enter into that abundant life.

Christ manifested love. He told His disciples how much He

loved them and the world: "Greater love hath no man than this, that a man lay down his life for his friends" (John 15:13). He loved God, He loved sinners, and He loved those who loved Him. In this epistle John reminds us that God is love and that we, too, have a responsibility to love. This is developed in chapters three and four.

Third, Jesus was obedient to the will of God. He testified, "I do always those things that please him" (John 8:29). John was in the Garden when He registered His complete obedience to the Father. "Not my will, but thine, be done." The obedience of Christ is reflected in the fifth chapter of John's epistle, where he shares the implications of the obedience of Christ for the child of God who would enter into the fullness of life.

Study Questions

1. Why does John write this epistle to his children?
2. What was John's relationship to the recipients of this letter?
3. Define the "abundant life" of which Christ speaks.
4. How had John learned about the abundant life?
5. What are the chief characteristics of abundant life?

2

THE FULLNESS OF JOY

1 John 1:3–4

IT IS DIFFICULT for a blind man to translate someone's description of an object into a mental picture; and it was also difficult for men to understand Jesus' description of His Father. Man's mind was darkened to God's power and deity revealed in creation. Men are in ignorance, and if that darkness is to be dispelled, they must learn from the Lord Jesus Christ what the Father is like. The Son translated the life of the Father into a life lived before men so that they could come to know the Father.

John writes: "That which we have seen and heard declare we unto you, that ye also may have fellowship with us: and truly our fellowship is with the Father, and with His Son Jesus Christ" (1 John 1:3). John refers to his readers over and over as his children; there was no estrangement between John and the Ephesians. He is not writing to heal a breach when he says, "That ye also may have fellowship with us." He is writing so that they might enjoy the same fellowship with the Father and the Son that he and the other apostles enjoyed. To paraphrase verse 3: "That which we have seen and heard about this abundant life we declare unto you that ye also may enjoy the same fellowship in this life that we do."

We are sometimes envious of those 12 men our Lord chose to be with Him. We would love to have stood where John stood, to see the Lord Jesus touch a blind eye so that sight is restored, or touch a casket and see the dead rise. We are envious that they heard our Lord teach them about the Father and the abundant life He had come to share with them. We somehow feel that we would be far ahead spiritually. Although the apostles saw Christ's deeds and heard His teachings, they did not understand them until after the Resurrection. We have the same capacity to enter into the abundant life available in Jesus Christ as any one of those men.

Jesus prophesied, "At that day ye shall know that I am in my Father, and ye in me, and I in you" (John 14:20). And the Lord said, "If a man love me, he will keep my words: and my Father will love him, and we will come unto him, and make our abode with him" (John 14:23). Twice in that chapter the Lord promised that these disciples, who had seen and heard so much without fully comprehending it, would finally enter into the fullness of life that He had come to share. Then He and the Father would dwell in them and they would dwell in Him and the Father.

John explains this fellowship in the latter part of the third verse. "Our fellowship is with the Father, and with His Son Jesus Christ." The word translated "fellowship" has in it the idea of having something in common. When two strangers are together in a situation where conversation seems necessary, they begin to probe to find some point of contact. "Where are you from?" "Where did you go to school?" "What is your hobby?" There is a wall between the two until they find some point of contact.

And before an individual can have fellowship with the Father and the Son, there must be some mutual point of contact. This is why God created men as He did.

> God said, Let us make man in our image, after our likeness: and let them have dominion over the fish of the sea, and over the fowl of the air, and over the cattle, and over all the earth, and over every creeping thing that creepeth upon the earth. So God created man in his own image, in the image of God created he him. (Gen. 1:26–27).

Four times it is stated that God created man in His own image. Man was the capstone of all of God's creative work. Man reflects God's person.

God possesses the capacity of intellect to such an infinite degree that He knows all things. He possesses the capacity of emotion; so John could write, "God so loved the world, that he gave his only begotten Son." God possesses a will with which He can choose and act—He is sovereign. There are no deficiencies in God's personality and He possesses all of these capacities to an infinite degree.

When God created Adam He did not make an animal. He made a person, and God gave Adam a mind to receive truth and to respond to that truth and know God. He gave Adam emotions so that he could receive the love of God and respond to God. He gave Adam a will so that when he received a revelation of the will of God he might respond and submit to the will of God. Adam had to a limited degree the same capacity that God possessed in infinite degree. Adam was in perfect fellowship with God.

But Adam disobeyed and darkness settled on his mind so that he could not understand the truth of God; his emotions were degraded so that he could not love God; and his will was deadened so that he could not obey God. Adam lost all point of contact so that fellowship between Adam and the Creator was impossible.

To make fellowship possible, the Lord Jesus Christ came into this world to make man a new creation. God imparts to the one who receives Christ as personal Savior a new mind so that he can understand and respond to the truth of God. He gives a new capacity of emotion so that he can receive and respond to the love of God. He gives a new will so that he can receive a revelation of the will of God and obey the will of God. John is speaking of the response of the total person to the total person of the Father and the Son.

John shares with them again in verse 4 his reason for writing.

"These things write we unto you, that your joy may be full." John knows that the only true joy a child of God can experience is the joy that comes from being rightly related to the Father and the Son. This joy is exemplified by the Lord Jesus Christ.

Christ's joy did not come from this world's goods. He warned those who wanted to be His disciples : "The foxes have holes, and the birds of the air have nests; but the Son of man hath not where to lay His head" (Matt. 8:20). He lived on a subpoverty level. When it came time to pay taxes, the Lord Jesus sent Peter to catch a fish and there find a coin to pay the taxes of two people; He slept in the homes of those who extended hospitality, yet He knew infinite joy.

The world never heaped accolades on Jesus. His own people called Him a blasphemous traitor. He was not a business success. He was not a free man, for He was born among people enslaved to Rome. His joy resulted from being one with the Father and possessing the life of the Father.

As John's children look for spiritual satisfaction, they will not find it in what they accomplish or acquire. They will find joy in relationship with God, the source of abundant life.

Study Questions

1. How did Christ reveal the Father?
2. What was the purpose of this revelation?
3. What does it mean to be in the image of God?
4. What is fellowship with God?
5. How does a believer enter into joy?

3

FELLOWSHIP AND HOLINESS

1 John 1:5–7a

THE HOSTS IN HEAVEN worship God continuously because of the perfection of His person. Isaiah saw the seraphim surrounding the throne of God and heard them saying, "Holy, holy, holy, is the LORD of Hosts" (6:3). God Himself finds His greatest delight in, and is justifiably proud of, His perfection. His character is holy. His thought is holy. His speech is holy. His acts are holy. While God is worthy to be revered for each of His attributes, heaven magnifies Him above all because of the perfection of His person.

It is impossible for such a God to receive into His presence those who do not measure up to His character. But God makes men acceptable to Himself through Jesus Christ. However, God cannot fellowship with one who is redeemed unless that person is walking in holiness.

John begins writing to his children in the faith by reminding them of the holiness of God. To fellowship with the Father they must know the basis of fellowship, as revealed by Christ: "This then is the message which we have heard of him, and declare unto you, that God is light, and in him is no darkness at all" (v. 5). Darkness and light are diametrically opposed, where light shines there is no darkness and where darkness is, there is no light.

John is using a figure employed throughout Scripture to depict

21

the absolute holiness of God. After creation by the word of God, the earth was without form and void, empty and useless, and "darkness was upon the face of the deep" (Gen. 1:2). God banished the darkness by bringing light. He said, "Let there be light: and there was light" (Gen. 1:3). That light did not originate in a heavenly sun, it originated in a Person, the person of the Creator. The Creator dispelled the darkness with His presence before light ever emanated from the sun.

In obedience to the command of God Moses raised up the tabernacle, preparing and placing the furniture in accordance with God's revealed instructions. And the Holy of Holies was wrapped in darkness because God had given no instructions for illuminating the recesses of the tabernacle. God brought the light of His presence to dispel the darkness. When all was in order, "a cloud covered the tent of the congregation, and the glory of the LORD filled the tabernacle. And Moses was not able to enter into the tent of the congregation, because the cloud abode thereon, and the glory of the LORD filled the tabernacle" (Exod. 40:34–35). God caused a veil to be placed between the Holy of Holies and a guilty people lest they be consumed by the brightness of His glory.

In obedience to his father's instructions, Solomon built a magnificent temple of costly hewn stones and overlaid with gold and encrusted with silver; but there is no record of a window in that edifice. Once again the light of God's holiness dispelled the darkness. We read "And it came to pass, when the priests were come out of the holy place, that the cloud filled the house of the LORD, so that the priests could not stand to minister because of the cloud: for the glory of the LORD had filled the house of the LORD" (1 Kings 8:10–11). The priests carried no lamp, for they walked in the light of the holiness of God.

In the first chapter of John's Gospel the world is again wrapped in darkness—spiritual darkness. God had revealed Himself to men, but they had rejected the light to walk in darkness. They had become blind because they did not know God. "All things were made by him; and without him was not any thing made that was made. In him was life; and the life was the light of men. And the light shineth in darkness; and the darkness comprehended it not'' (John 1:3–5). Jesus came into the world to dispel the darkness in the minds and hearts of men. "That [He] was the true Light, which lighteth every man that cometh into the world" (John 1:9).

Light has properties that help us understand God's holiness and his fellowship with men. First of all, light reveals. If something is lost, you use light to find it. When God's revelation to men was lost because of the blindness of the natural mind, Jesus Christ came as the Light, revealing the person of a holy God. Christ says, "No man hath seen God at any time; the only begotten Son, which is in the bosom of the Father, he hath declared [revealed] him" (John 1:18).

Light also purifies. I remember when our family doctor told us it was no longer necessary to keep my brother in isolation. I could move back into the room we shared. How I dreaded returning to a room once contaminated by scarlet fever! The doctor said we should take every item in the room out into the sunlight; so I helped my mother carry mattresses, carpets, drapes, and empty drawers down the stairs and outside where we spread them on the grass. After these items had been purified by the light of the sun, I was able to lie down and sleep in that room without fear of contamination.

It is also the peculiar property of light that it cannot be contaminated. There is no such thing as dirty light. Some of the sunlight may not be able to enter a room because the window is dirty, but the light that does pass through will not be affected by the dirt.

John is using an apt figure to convey a God of perfection who cannot be defiled. He reveals and purifies the uncleanness in us, but He is not contaminated.

Finally, light also comforts. What parent has not been awakened in the middle of the night by the fearful cry of a child? The parent slips in and dispels the fear by turning on a light. The light brings comfort and rest. Man knows only fear of the Almighty because he is ignorant of God and anticipates God's judgment. Jesus is the God of all comfort. The Lord Jesus Christ came to let the light of the knowledge of God shine in the hearts of men.

Salvation through Christ, the Light, does not make fellowship with God automatic. "If we say that we have fellowship with him, and walk in darkness, we lie, and do not the truth" (v. 6).

If God were to fellowship with us while we are in sin, He would involve Himself in our sin. The one who sits behind the wheel of the getaway car is as much a bank robber as his partner inside the bank holding the gun. Adam sinned and ran to hide in the shadow of a bush. God came to fellowship with Adam, but He did not go down into the shadows. He stood in the light and said, "Adam, where art thou?" Adam was not restored to fellowship until God had slain an animal and covered Adam's nakedness with the skin, thereby covering his sin with the blood.

In verse 7 John makes clear that the prerequisite to fellowship is to walk in the light. "If we walk in the light, as he is in the light, we have fellowship one with another" (v. 7). John is not talking about the fellowship of two believers. He is referring to a believer in fellowship with the Father and the Son. The believer must be living in the light of the holiness of God, without any flaw in thought or word or deed, to fellowship with the Father and the Son. Our salvation does not depend on our godliness, but our fellowship with the Father does.

Peter also learned this truth from hearing the words of the Lord and from observing Him. "But as he which hath called you is holy, so be ye holy in all manner of conversation [life]; because it is written, Be ye holy; for I am holy" (1 Peter 1:15–16).

A holy God cannot tolerate sin. To know the blessing of fellowship with God and then step into darkness and walk alone is to rob yourself of joyful companionship with the Lord.

Study Questions

1. Define the holiness of God.
2. What does God's holiness require of those who would fellowship with Him?
3. Explain John's use of the figure *light*.
4. Why is Christ called the light of the world?
5. Why is it impossible for God to fellowship with a sinner?

4

THE VALUE OF THE BLOOD
OF CHRIST

1 John 1:7b–10

THE HEART OF THE BELIEVER confirms the testimony of Scripture—
we were born in sin, we have practiced sin, and even though we
have been redeemed we still have the capacity to sin. How can a
holy God fellowship with a redeemed child who does sin? John
comes face to face with this problem in his epistle.

Count Von Zinzendorf wrote,

> Lord, I believe Thy precious blood
> Which at the mercy seat of God,
> Forever doth for sinners plead,
> For me, e'en for my soul was shed.

Von Zinzendorf grasped the truth that John states so plainly in
verse 7: fellowship with God is possible because of the lasting
worth of the blood of Jesus Christ. The blood of Jesus Christ keeps
on cleansing us from all sin.

Throughout Scripture God reveals the redemptive value of
blood. When the children of Israel were in bondage in Egypt, God
fulfilled His promise and delivered them. God sentenced all of the
firstborn in Egypt to death:

> Thus saith the LORD, About midnight will I go out into the
> midst of Egypt: and all the firstborn in the land of Egypt shall

27

die, from the firstborn of Pharaoh that sitteth upon his throne, even unto the firstborn of the maidservant that is behind the mill; and all the firstborn of beasts. And there shall be a great cry throughout all the land of Egypt, such as there was none like it, nor shall be like it any more (Exod. 11:4–6).

God also provided an escape from that universal death sentence: ''And the blood shall be to you, for a token upon the houses where ye are: and when I see the blood, I will pass over you, and the plague shall not be upon you to destroy you, when I smite the land of Egypt'' (Exod. 12:13). Those who believed God placed the blood of a lamb on their doorposts.

The word translated "pass over" has several meanings. One meaning is to "leap by." The death angel would by-pass the house with blood on the doorposts. The word also has in it the thought of hovering over: "When I see the blood, I will hover over you." The blood brought God's protection to that household. God, the judge, now became the protector against the death angel. The death angel passed by because God was there to turn him aside. The blood brought a deliverer who charged Himself with the responsibility of protecting one who was under judgment. "Pass over" has in it the idea of a personal defender who protects those who acted in faith. The blood brought a deliverer.

The writer of Hebrews speaks of the value of blood: "This is the blood of the testament which God hath enjoined unto you. Moreover, he sprinkled with blood both the tabernacle, and all the vessels of the ministry. And almost all things are by the law purged with blood; and without shedding of blood is no remission" (Heb. 9:20–22).

''Without the shedding of blood is no remission'' refers to a ritual in the Day of Atonement.

> Then shall he kill the goat of the sin offering, that is for the people, and bring his blood within the veil, and do with that blood as he did with the blood of the bullock, and sprinkle it upon the mercy seat, and before the mercy seat: and he shall make an atonement for the holy place, because of the un-

cleanness of the children of Israel, and because of their transgressions in all their sins: and so shall he do for the tabernacle of the congregation, that remaineth among them in the midst of their uncleanness (Lev. 16:15–16).

The high priest entered the Holy of Holies with the blood of an animal sacrifice and sprinkled the blood on the mercy seat. Above the mercy seat dwelt the Shekinah glory of God, the visible sign of God's presence among His people. Beneath the mercy seat in the Ark was the Law given to Moses. The Law had been broken, necessitating a blood sacrifice. So the blood on the mercy seat was between God and a broken law, literally covering sin.

On the Day of Atonement the people pleaded for mercy after confessing they were guilty and deserved judgment. God permitted the high priest to sprinkle the blood on the mercy seat and cover the iniquity of the people for another twelve months.

God had designated appropriate sacrifices for the Israelite who had sinned in ignorance, but there was no prescribed sacrifice for the Israelite guilty of premeditated sin. However, the child of God who had sinned willfully could remind God that the blood was on the mercy seat and then ask God's forgiveness.

David had sinned heinously, but he confessed his sin when he prayed: "Have mercy upon me, O God, according to thy lovingkindness: according unto the multitude of thy tender mercies blot out my transgressions. Wash me thoroughly from mine iniquity, and cleanse me from my sin. For I acknowledge my transgressions: and my sin is ever before me" (Ps. 51:1–3), Then he pleaded, "Purge me with hyssop, and I shall be clean: wash me, and I shall be whiter than snow" (Ps. 51:7). On the Day of Atonement the high priest used a hyssop branch to sprinkle the blood on the mercy seat. So David is pleading that this blood cover his sin. Later he joyfully sings, "Blessed is he whose transgression is forgiven, whose sin is covered" (Ps. 32:1).

In obedience to the will of God the sinless, eternal Son of God shed His blood to cover sin forever. A literal translation of 1 John

1:7 reads, "The blood of Jesus Christ, God's Son, keeps on cleansing us from all sin." Though it was shed nearly two thousand years ago, the blood of Christ has full power to cleanse. Fellowship with God is possible because of the lasting worth of the blood of Jesus Christ.

John treats misconceptions about the basis of fellowship between the child and his Father in verses 8 and 10. Some might say that fellowship with God is possible because man has lost his sin nature. An Irish pastor told me of a man who said, "Pastor Mullen, I have not sinned in thirty years." The pastor gasped, "You haven't sinned in thirty years?" "No, I haven't." Mullen replied, "Brother, keep it up for four more years and you'll have preeminence in heaven, because the Lord Jesus only lived thirty-three years without sinning."

John denies that we attain a state of perfection in this life. Paraphrasing verse 8, we read: "If we say that we no longer have a sin nature, we deceive ourselves, and the truth is not in us." Satan would like us to believe that we are beyond his power to tempt, and thus become easy prey when we let down our guard. The sin nature is ever with us. Fellowship with the Father is not the result of attaining a state of holiness in this life.

Paraphrasing verse 10 reveals a second misconception. "If we say that what we did was not really sin, we make God a liar and His Word is not in us." For some people sin is heinous wrongdoing such as murder or adultery, rather than the waywardness that plagues most of us day after day. But only God can define sin. Fellowship with the Father does not result from redefining sin and making God a liar by winking at anything unlike His absolute holiness.

Verse 9 states the principle whereby the death of Christ covers our sins so that we may regain fellowship. "If we confess our sins, he is faithful and just to forgive us our sins, and to cleanse us from all unrighteousness." "We" refers to the family of believers. When the believer sins, the blood of Christ is instantaneously,

automatically applied to the believer (v. 7), maintaining his sonship with the Father, but sin has broken fellowship. My child may
strain our relationship by disobeying, but he is still my child.
Disobedience does not affect position, it affects fellowship. To be
restored to fellowship with God we must confess our sin.

Confession is not generalizing before we drop off to sleep, "If
I've done anything bad today, forgive me." The word *confess*
means to say the same thing that God says about our sin. God
points a finger at sin and says, "That was sin." When the Spirit of
God illuminates our minds so that we judge our sin as God judges
it, without making an excuse and without attempting to cover up,
then we have made confession. Confession is to say, "Father, I
have sinned." This is difficult for us because we like to defend
ourselves, to excuse ourselves, to rationalize our sinfulness and so
avoid God's assessment of sin. The prodigal son's first words to
his father were, "Father, I have sinned." He was restored on the
basis of that confession.

If believers confess their sin, God is faithful and just to forgive
us. God is faithful to Himself and to His Word in that He places
confessed sin under the blood of Christ. He is just in that He
forgives His children's sins because of the everlasting value of the
blood of Christ. God deals with sin on only one basis—the blood
of Christ. We could also say that the one who has been cleansed is
no longer in darkness, he is in the light and can have fellowship
with the Father and the Son.

Sometimes God must lay a heavy hand on His child to confront
him with the sin hiding the face of God from him. If a child of God
harbors sin, God will chasten and scourge him to bring him to
confession. Then His beloved are cleansed and restored to fellowship. The most dangerous step to take is the first step out of
fellowship, because God will not allow His child to remain in
darkness. He will discipline His own to bring them to confession.

Study Questions

1. What is the basis of a believer's fellowship?
2. Why is blood valuable in God's sight?
3. Show from David's experience the value of blood.
4. Does the holiness of God demand the eradication of the sin nature before fellowship becomes possible?
5. What is the relationship of confession to fellowship?

5

OUR ADVOCATE

1 John 2:1–2

SINCE JOHN IS WRITING to introduce the abundant life that the Lord Jesus lived, he wants his children to live sinless lives. So John writes in verse 1, "My little children, these things write I unto you, that ye sin not." The sinlessness of Christ was attested to by all who touched His life. The angel announced to Mary, "That holy thing which shall be born of thee shall be called the Son of God" (Luke 1:35). When face to face with the Lord, demons cried out, "I know thee who thou art; the Holy One of God" (Luke 4:34). Peter, who knew Him intimately, said Christ "did no sin, neither was guile found in his mouth" (1 Peter 2:22). At Christ's trial, six times the presiding judge declared Him to be innocent. The believer might conclude that sin is of little consequence because the blood of Christ restores us to fellowship with God. He might reason, If I sin God will apply the blood of Christ to my sin, maintaining me in positional relationship to Him and restoring me to fellowship with Him, so it really doesn't matter whether I sin or not.

To protect us from such erroneous thinking, John tells us in verses 1–2 what is involved when a believer sins. "If any man sin, we have an advocate with the Father, Jesus Christ the righteous: and he is the propitiation for our sins: and not for ours only, but also for the sins of the whole world." John draws back the curtain of heaven to show what happens when a child of God sins.

"If any man sin," might be translated, "While any man is still in the act of sinning." The believer's sin causes activity in heaven that is beyond human comprehension. While any man is in the act of sinning he has an advocate with the Father, Jesus Christ the righteous. "Advocate" is the word still used in England meaning defense attorney. It is meaningful to read the clause that way, "While any man is sinning, we have a defense attorney." A defense attorney becomes necessary when someone has been charged with wrongdoing. So the sinning child of God has been accused. God will not accuse the believer because God sees him not in his sin but in Jesus Christ. "If God be for us, who can be against us? He that spared not his own Son, but delivered him up for us all, how shall he not with him also freely give us all things? Who shall lay any thing to the charge of God's elect? It is God that justifieth" (Rom. 8:31–33). Jesus Christ is not the accuser because "it is Christ that died, yea rather, that is risen again, who is even at the right hand of God, who also maketh intercession for us" (Rom. 8:34).

The accuser is identified in Revelation 12:10: "Now is come salvation, and strength, and the kingdom of our God, and the power of his Christ: for the accuser of our brethren is cast down, which accused them before our God day and night." While Christ acts as our defense attorney, Satan stands before God as the constant accuser of the brethren.

The Book of Job illustrates this. God testifies that Job is a righteous man, a child of God by faith. He is a diligent priest in his family, offering worship and sacrifice to God. God is well pleased with those sacrifices, but Satan is displeased and seeks to discredit Job. He accuses Job of worshiping God in order to receive God's blessings. The book unfolds to show the tests and the trials of a righteous man and the ultimate triumph of faith over the accusations of the evil one.

Satan is engaged in a struggle for the soul. Every believer was born into Satan's kingdom and served him until God reached down in His infinite grace and delivered him from bondage to Satan and brought him into His family as His child. Satan resents that the believer has been wrested from his authority and control. Seeking to enslave the believer again, the devil uses God's words, "The soul that sinneth, it shall die" (Ezek. 18:4) and "The wages of sin is death" (Rom. 6:23). He has the effrontery to say, "Look at what that believer is doing. I demand You return him to me."

God does not deliver us to Satan because of the plea of the defense attorney. This Advocate does not enter a plea of innocence, nor does He plead for mercy. He pleads on the basis of His own blood.

John states that this Advocate is "the propitiation for our sins." The word *propitiation* means to cover over, to put under blood. It refers to the Day of Atonement in the Old Testament when the high priest sprinkled the blood of an animal sacrifice on the mercy seat. That was a propitiatory sacrifice, a sacrifice that covered the broken law (see p. 29). John explains that Jesus Christ has offered His own blood as a sacrifice to God. His blood is a cover, providing safety and refuge for those under His blood.

Now God is propitious, dealing with believers on the basis of that blood. As the defense attorney, Christ can plead His righteousness, for He became sin for us that we might be made the righteousness of God (2 Cor. 5:21). The perfection of His person is transferred to our account.

The blood of Christ is sufficient for all sins, those of the believer as well as the unbeliever, for John adds, "He is the propitiation . . . not for ours only, but also for the sins of the whole world" (v. 3). In the sight of God the blood of Christ is of such limitless value that it cannot be depleted. It is sufficient to cover every sin of every person who has lived or will live. We cannot exhaust the value of the blood of Christ by putting ourselves under its protecting covering again and again.

Every time we sin, Christ must appear before God as our defense attorney to plead our cause. Such is His love and His infinite grace that the moment the believer sins, before he can even ask Him, Christ appears as our defense attorney to plead the infinite value of His blood. Then God the Father applies the blood of Christ to that sin so that we are maintained as sons of God.

> There is a fountain filled with blood,
>   Drawn from Immanuel's veins.
> And sinners plunged beneath that flood,
>   Lose all their guilty stains.

Study Questions

1. Why do believers need an advocate?
2. On what basis does our Advocate plead for our restoration?
3. What kind of an advocate do we have?
4. What does "propitiation" mean?
5. What is the practical value of Christ's work as Advocate for the believer?

6
OBEDIENCE AND FELLOWSHIP

1 John 2:3–6

THE FIRST EPISTLE OF JOHN provides a test of our fellowship with God: "Hereby we do know that we know him, if we keep his commandments." "Know him" is more than knowing we are saved, it is knowing that we are abiding in Christ. Obedience, then, determines whether we are in intimate fellowship with God the Father, God the Son, and God the Holy Spirit. Obedience is the basis of and the prerequisite to the believer's joy. There can be no happiness or contentment in the home until children are in this right relationship to their parents. There can be no right relationship in the classroom until the pupils are in this relationship to the teacher. There can be no contentment in society until citizens are in this relationship to those who have been put in authority over them. There can be no peace and contentment in the business world until employees are in this relationship to their employer. In every sphere in which we find ourselves, God has ordained authority and that institution of authority demands submission. Submission involves obedience. And in the things of God, there can be no peace or contentment until those who are God's own are in subjection to His authority. Since we are by nature rebels, a problem arises. It is that problem of inherent disobedience that John treats in this passage.

John first states this proposition negatively in verse 4. "He that saith, I know him, and keepeth not his commandments, is a liar, and the truth is not in him." If the believer claims that he is abiding in Christ but is disobedient to His commandments, he is a liar. If a man says, "Lord Jesus, I love You for dying on the cross for me" but then disobeys His teachings in Scripture, his actions prove him to be a liar. Disobedience always disrupts and destroys.

John then states the same proposition positively in verse 5. "Whoso keepeth his word, in him verily is the love of God perfected: hereby know we that we are in him." If I am obeying the Word of God, then I am abiding with Christ.

The Lord Himself proclaimed this truth. "If a man love me, he will keep my words: and my Father will love him, and we will come unto him, and make our abode with him. . . . and the word which ye hear is not mine, but the Father's which sent me" (John 14:23–24). This teaching of Jesus is the foundation for John's discourse here.

The test of fellowship with God, then, is what we do in obedience to His instructions in His Word. The believer who loves God wants to please Him and shuns displeasing Him.

Christ also reinforced this truth in somewhat different terms. "As the Father hath loved me, so have I loved you: continue ye in my love. If ye keep my commandments, ye shall abide in my love; even as I have kept my Father's commandments, and abide in his love" (John 15:9–10). Jesus' love for His Father expressed itself in absolute obedience, and the infinite love of the Father could flow to the Son because He was obedient. John speaks of this kind of obedience in verse 5. "Whoso keepeth his word, in him verily is the love of God perfected: hereby know we that we are in him."

In verse 6 John has given us an example of what it is to live a life of obedience so that God can flood the life with joy. "He that saith he abideth in him ought himself also so to walk, even as he walked." If you want an example of a life of joy that is a result of complete obedience, there is only one place you can look, and that is to the Lord Jesus. The person who says he is abiding in Christ must be walking in complete obedience, as Jesus Christ walked.

How did Jesus walk? A good illustration of this is found in John's Gospel. The Lord Jesus made a great affirmation when He said, "I am the light of the world" (John 8:12). The darkness that had settled upon the world was a result of ignorance of God. The world "by wisdom knew not God" (1 Cor. 1:21). Consequently their minds were blinded to the truth. Jesus Christ came to reveal the Father to men. His revelation of the Father was light in darkness and He was the revealer of light to men.

On this occasion, our Lord stood before a vast multitude and said to them, "I will make the Father known to you so that your ignorance and your darkness are dispelled." Christ was immediately challenged by the Pharisees, "Thou bearest record of thyself; thy record is not true" (v. 13). In verse 18 the Lord replied to that rejection, "The Father that sent me beareth witness of me." In verse 19 Christ is challenged again, "Then said they unto him, Where is thy Father?" And the Lord replied by saying that He was going to the Father. His acceptance into the Father's presence was proof of His person. Finally they retorted, "Who are you?" Jesus replied, "Even the same that I said unto you from the beginning."

When the Pharisees would not believe that He was the Son of God, Jesus stated that His obedience to the Father proved His deity. "I do always those things that please him" (John 8:29). Never in thought, or word, or deed had He displeased the Father. Christ's obedience convinced the multitude gathered around Him and the Pharisees that He was the Son of God come to reveal the Father. "As he spake these words, many believed on him" (John 8:30).

The world has its standards of conduct, and in these days we have new revelations as to just how far men stray from the standards of the Word of God. Men in high places believe they can live on a plane of morality radically different from the standard for which the rest of us hold ourselves responsible.

When we adopt the standards of the world, we will never conform to God's holy demands and joyfully obey His Word. In the midst of the world's flexible standard is the inflexible standard of the Word of God, revealing the demands of God's absolute holiness. God fellowships with His children on the basis of His unalterable, holy character. "Thus saith the Lord" is the basis of fellowship and the ground of the believer's joy.

Study Questions

1. What is the relationship of obedience to fellowship?
2. Why is obedience necessary for fellowship?
3. What is the biblical concept of obedience?
4. What is the relationship of love and obedience?
5. What proof of His relationship to the Father did Christ give His enemies?

7

LOVE AND FELLOWSHIP

1 John 2:7–11

GOD REVEALS HIMSELF in His Word as a God of love. To fellowship with a God of love, one must walk in love. In 1 John 2:3–6 the apostle writes that the intimate fellowship that will bring the believer into the fullness of joy depends first of all on obedience. Verses 7–11 relate that intimate fellowship with the Father and the Son also depends on loving one's brother.

Loving one's brother is introduced in verse 7 by linking it with the Old Testament. One of the fundamental postulates of the Mosaic law was that the Israelites were to love one another. The righteousness that the law demanded would be manifested in loving one's neighbor as well as in loving God.

The Pharisees, a sect claiming to interpret the law of Moses, sent a hostile representative to test Jesus. The Pharisees had codified the Old Testament law into 365 prohibitions and 250 commandments and a man supposedly discharged his responsibility to God by observing all of these.

The Pharisee challenged Christ: "If you are what you claim to be, sent from God, tell us what the greatest commandment in the law is." This was tantamount to asking Christ what the purpose of the law was, and how one fulfilled the demands of righteousness in the law. The Lord replied: "Thou shalt love the Lord thy God with all thy heart, and with all thy soul, and with all thy mind. This is the first and great commandment. And the second is like unto it, Thou shalt love thy neighbor as thyself'' (Matt. 22:37–39).

According to Jesus, the purpose of the law was to fulfill the righteousness of God. God's people manifested His righteousness first of all by loving God, and second, by loving their neighbor. This was the old commandment woven throughout the Word of God.

When Jesus gathered His disciples around Him in the upper room, He said to them: "By this shall all men know that ye are my disciples, if ye have love one to another" (John 13:35). The people of Israel had many marks of identification. Circumcision indicated belief in God's covenant with Abraham and keeping the Sabbath day was evidence of receiving the Mosaic law. The disciples of the Pharisees were easily recognized because they placed portions of Scripture in little boxes tied to their foreheads or forearms. Those phylacteries were a sign of their submission to the teachings of the Pharisees. Those who identified themselves with John the Baptist received his baptism. Every one of these marks was external.

In the upper room the Lord told His disciples that He would give them an internal mark of identification. Their mark would be their love for one another.

Later in this upper room discourse, Jesus elaborated on loving one another:

> As the Father hath loved me, so have I loved you: continue ye [abide] in my love. If ye keep my commandments, ye shall abide in my love; even as I have kept my Father's commandments, and abide in his love. These things have I spoken unto you, that my joy might remain in you, and that your joy might be full. This is my commandment, That ye love one another, as I have loved you. Greater love hath no man than this, that a man lay down his life for his friends. Ye are my friends, if ye do whatsoever I command you. . . . These things I command you, that ye love one another" (John 15:9–14,17).

After saying in verse 7 that he was not writing a new commandment but an old commandment, John then speaks of "a new commandment" (v. 8). This new commandment is the Old Testament instruction that the Lord Jesus Christ emphasized in the upper room when He said to His disciples, "This is my commandment, That ye love one another."

Building on the concept of loving one's brother, the apostle Paul speaks of love fulfilling the law. "Owe no man any thing, but to love one another: for he that loveth another hath fulfilled the law" (Rom. 13:8). Paul explains that those seeking the highest good of their brother will never transgress the law, for breaking of the law is never love. "Love worketh no ill to his neighbor: therefore love is the fulfilling of the law" (Rom. 13:10).

In verses 9–11 John makes it clear that fellowship with God depends on love for the brother. Without love for the brother there can be no love for God. And where there is no love for God there is no fellowship with the Father and the Son. In verse 9 the one who claims to be in the light but is hating his brother is actually in darkness. Such cannot under any circumstance be enjoying fellowship with God. Where there is hate, there is no fellowship. Where there is hate, there is no joy.

The biblical concept of hate is not so much an act as it is an attitude. When I am not demonstrating affection for the brother, I am hating the brother. Since John wants to lead his children into the fullness of joy, he commands them to love. For fellowship depends on love for the brethren, and where there is no love, one is in hate and fellowship and joy are impossible.

The love of which John speaks is not so much a manifestation of the emotions as it is a manifestation of the will. The love that John writes about is not first of all an emotional response to another person. It is an interest in, care for, and concern about another person. The love of God for the sinner was demonstrated. "God so loved the world, that he gave his only begotten Son" (John 3:16). God recognized that the greatest need of the sinner was a solution to the sin problem, and because God sought the highest good of those whom He loved He sent His Son to be the sacrifice for our sins that through His death we might have life. This was an act, not so much of God's emotions, but of God's will because He sought the highest good of the sinner. And the love that makes fellowship with God possible and engulfs the child of God in the fullness of joy is a care and a concern about the need of another person.

A key word in this matter is the word *commitment*. Loving the brother demands the commitment of a person to a person. When one believer shows care and concern about the total needs of a brother in Christ as a person, he is fulfilling the obligation of Scripture to love a brother. Too often we conclude that if we write out a check to cover a brother's material needs we have discharged our obligation to him. That is but an insignificant part.

A person can attend a church and can send his check to meet the bills and pay the salaries and maintain the properties, and feel he has discharged his commitment to the church. All he has done is take care of housekeeping details. A church is not a group of people committed to a building or to an organization. When people become members of a church they are making a commitment to each other. And not until we exercise the responsibilities of that personal commitment one to the other are we functioning as a church. We must minister one to the other, bear one another's burdens, share one another's griefs, support one another in need, minister one to the other in love.

If I hurt and have deep needs, but out of pride I refuse to share those needs with you, what I am saying to you is, "I don't love you." And when we are acquainted with needs and refuse to respond, we are saying, "I don't love you." We cannot then enjoy fullness of fellowship with the Father and with the Son.

We like to withdraw into our own little circle and build a wall around ourselves. We can do that, but then we will not know the fullness of joy that comes from loving the brethren. "Hereby shall all men know ye are my disciples, if ye . . . love." If you would know the fullness of joy, love the brethren, and so fulfill the law of Christ.

Study Questions

1. What demands did the law of Moses make on those who desired to please God?
2. How did Christ's command to love differ from Moses' command?
3. Why is love a proof of one's relationship to Christ?
4. How is love a fulfillment of the law?
5. What is the biblical concept of love?

8

YOUR SINS ARE FORGIVEN

1 John 2:12–14

IT IS AN ALMOST UNBELIEVABLE FACT that we can have intimate fellowship with God. That God desires fellowship with His creatures is utterly astounding, for when we recognize the judgment of Scripture, "all have sinned, and come short of the glory of God" (Rom. 3:23), we cannot but wonder why God would desire to fellowship with us.

In 1 John 2:12–14, three statements show us the basis for this fellowship. He writes in verse 12, "Your sins are forgiven you." In verses 13 and 14 he says, "Ye have known him that is from the beginning." And in the same two verses he writes, "Ye have overcome the wicked one."

This fellowship with the Father is not limited to one age group nor to one group who have reached a certain spiritual standing. John addresses these words to fathers, young men, and little children. Fellowship is possible from the youngest to the oldest.

He is also emphasizing that fellowship is not reserved for those who have come to spiritual maturity. It is not only for those who are fathers in the faith but also for those who are young in the faith and those who are newborn babes in Christ. This privilege of intimate fellowship with the Father is possible to any child of God.

First of all, John says, "I write unto you, little children, because your sins are forgiven you for his name's sake" (v. 12). The word *forgive* means to remove, to erase, to put away. It has in it the idea of the separation of the sinner and his sin so that one is no longer identified with the other.

To one familiar with the Old Testament, this brings to mind the ritual of the Day of Atonement. On that annual feast day, observed according to the law by Israel, on behalf of the nation the high priest sacrificed two goats. When the first was slain, the high priest took the basin filled with blood into the Holy of Holies and sprinkled it on the mercy seat. The mercy seat covered the ark, which contained the law Israel had violated. Above the mercy seat resided the Shekinah glory of God, the visible representation of God's presence among the people of Israel. The high priest interposed blood between a holy God who must judge a sinful people and the law that condemned them.

The high priest then left the Holy of Holies and placed his hands on the head of the second goat, confessing the sins of the nation. Then he entrusted the animal to a man responsible to lead it into the wilderness.

As a member of the congregation saw the priest placing his hands on the head of the goat, he could think: "My sins are being transferred to a substitute. That goat is my sin-bearer." Then he would watch the animal being led out of the camp, and he could say, "The sins that I bore, that animal now bears, and he is bearing them away from me so that I no longer bear them." As he watched the man disappear over the horizon, he could say, "My sins have been removed; my sins are gone."

That separation of the sin from the sinner is the fundamental concept in the mind of the apostle when he says, "Your sins are forgiven you for his name's sake." God, in the Old Testament, had promised the coming of a Savior who would provide forgiveness of sin. In giving Israel a new covenant God promised, "For I will forgive their iniquity, and I will remember their sin no more"

(Jer. 31:34). Quoting that passage, the writer to the Hebrews states, "This is the covenant that I will make with them after those days, saith the Lord, I will put my laws into their hearts, and in their minds will I write them; and their sins and iniquities will I remember no more. Now where remission [putting away, removal] of these is, there is no more offering for sin" (Heb. 10:16–18).

Thus John has emphasized that Jesus Christ came into this world specifically to make it possible for God to remove sin from the sinner. There is no happier message in the Word of God than this good news that our sins have been erased, not only from the record of God, but from the very memory of God. And because my sins have been forgiven, I can enjoy fellowship with God.

At the conclusion of the Last Supper Jesus took bread and said, "This is my body." And then He took the cup, gave thanks, and gave it to the disciples saying, "Drink ye all of it; for this is my blood of the new testament [covenant], which is shed for many for the remission [putting away, forgiveness] of sins" (Matt. 26: 27–28). As He passed the cup to the disciples He was saying, "This is to remind you that my blood was spilled so that your sins might be removed from my memory forever." Fellowship is possible because of the forgiveness of sins.

In verse 13 and again in verse 14 John states, "I write unto you, fathers, because ye have known him that is from the beginning." There is a vast difference between knowing about a person and knowing him personally. Jesus Christ came into this world to introduce the Father to us and introduce us to the Father, so that knowing the Father, we might enjoy fellowship with Him. In John 1:18 the apostle wrote, "No man hath seen God at any time; the only begotten Son, which is in the bosom of the Father, he hath declared [revealed, introduced] him." Jesus emphasized the necessity of this introduction of the Father to us and us to the Father, "All things are delivered unto me of my Father: and no man knoweth the Son, but the Father; neither knoweth any man the

Father, save the Son, and he to whomsoever the Son will reveal him" (Matt. 11:27). Were it not for the revelation that Jesus Christ has given to us, we might as well place over our church entrances the Greek superscription, "To the Unknown God." Natural man does not come to know God by natural means. And natural man will never discover God and come to know Him so that he can enjoy Him. He may look at God's handiwork and be convinced that God exists and that He is a God of power who has arranged this universe, but he will never know Him personally. Jesus Christ came to make the unknown God known to man so we might enjoy fellowship with Him.

In his Gospel John records Philip questioning Jesus: "Lord, shew us the Father, and it sufficeth us. Jesus saith unto him, Have I been so long time with you, and yet hast thou not known me, Philip? he that hath seen me hath seen the Father; and how sayest thou then, Shew us the Father? Believest thou not that I am in the Father, and the Father in me? . . ." (John 14:8–10). What John had learned about the Father from Jesus brought him into intimate fellowship with the Father. John had taught his spiritual children and they had come to know the Father. Fellowship is possible not only because sins are forgiven, but also because believers come to know God as their Father.

Thirdly, John says, "Ye have overcome the wicked one." The believer has come through the territory over which Satan reigns.

I once looked out my study window and saw our dachshund under the pecan tree in our side yard, leaping as high as her little three-inch legs would allow. She was barking and growling at a squirrel calmly eating nuts on one of the limbs, oblivious to any noise or danger. The squirrel was secure up there where no dachshund could ever go, but to get there it had to run across the lawn and climb to safety. Until up in the tree, it was in jeopardy. The believer finds safety and security where God has placed him.

Paul refers to this when he says God has "delivered us from the power of darkness, and hath translated us into the kingdom of his dear Son: in whom we have redemption through his blood, even the forgiveness of sins'' (Col. 1:13–14). Paul brings the same facts together that John presented. God has provided blood as a covering for sin and the one who puts himself under that blood experiences the forgiveness of sins. When he enters into the blessings of sins forgiven, he is translated out of the kingdom of this world, the kingdom of Satan into which he had been born, and is lifted up into the kingdom of "His dear Son." All the ravages of Satan cannot dislodge him nor unsettle him because he is secure in the privileges that are his as a child of God.

Paul states in 2 Corinthians 2:14 that Christ always leads His own in His train of triumph. He is the Victor in a triumphal procession that will take Him into glory and He sweeps along in His train the multitudes who have received Him as Savior and have experienced the forgiveness of sin.

And we walk in His triumph. And because we are victors, we can enjoy fellowship with the Father. This intimate experience of enjoying the Father's presence is possible for us because our sins have been forgiven, because we have come to know the Father intimately through Jesus Christ and have been lifted out of that sphere where no fellowship is possible and have been brought into the family of God.

Study Questions

1. What is the relationship of "forgiveness of sins" to fellowship?
2. What is the relationship of "ye have known him" to fellowship?
3. What is the relationship of "ye have overcome the wicked one" to fellowship?
4. Is fellowship limited to any age group?
5. Is fellowship limited to mature believers?

9

LOVE FOR THE WORLD

1 John 2:15–17

NOT EVERY SCRIPTURAL COMMANDMENT is to be found in the Old Testament; many of the words of Jesus and His apostles constitute New Testament commandments. So John commands his spiritual children, "Love not the world."

The term "world" has three meanings in Scripture. At times it refers to the earth. God created the earth to reveal to men that He is God and the powerful Creator. The beauties of nature were designed to move men's hearts toward God and remind them of a Maker who wants His creatures to enjoy His rich creation. 1 John 2:15 does not employ this meaning of "world."

"World" frequently refers to the mass of mankind. But John is not forbidding love for the human race. Such a commandment would be contrary to God's character, for John 3:16 tells of a God who loves the world, the world of lost humanity, and who reached out in His love to provide a Savior. God would be countermanding His nature if believers were commanded not to love the mass of mankind whom He loves.

The most common use of "the world" in Scripture is to refer to the kingdom of Satan. Paul states that Satan is the god of this kingdom, "If our gospel be hid, it is hid to them that are lost: in whom the god of this world hath blinded the minds of them which believe not, lest the light of the glorious gospel of Christ, who is the image of God, should shine unto them'' (2 Cor. 4:3–4). The world under Satan also submits to his authority. 1 John 5:19 states, ''We know that we [the believer] are of God, and the whole world lieth in wickedness,'' or, literally, ''The whole world is cradled in the lap of the wicked one.''

This world is characterized by darkness. Paul says that God ''hath delivered us from the power of darkness, and hath translated us into the kingdom of his dear Son'' (1 Cor. 1:13). Darkness in Scripture is the absence of light and light is the knowledge of God. Satan's kingdom must walk in darkness because the god whom they recognize has eclipsed all knowledge of God.

Satan, the god of this world of darkness, is working out his purposes through his subjects, and this always produces disobedience because Satan is a rebel who is opposed to God. As a result, his subjects are opponents of God who walk in disobedience. ''Who were dead in trespasses and sins; wherein in time past ye walked according to the course of this world [according to the standards, the patterns of this world], according to the prince of the power of the air, the spirit that now worketh in the children of disobedience'' (Eph. 2:1–2). He expands on this in Ephesians 5, where he calls unbelievers enemies of God who war against His authority.

Christ characterized the world by its hatred of God: ''If the world hate you, ye know that it hated me before it hated you. If ye were of the world, the world would love his own: but because ye are not of the world, but I have chosen you out of the world, therefore the world hateth you'' (John 15:18–19).

The darkness and disobedience and hatred of the world result from its evil presuppositions. Paul uses the term ''wisdom'' for these presuppositions, ''My speech and my preaching was not with enticing words of man's wisdom, . . . that your faith should not stand in the wisdom of men. . . . yet not the wisdom of this world, nor of the princes of this world, that come to nought''

(1 Cor. 2:4). These presuppositions, established by Satan, are the foundation for the evil deeds of the kingdom of darkness.

This world system has its own organization. God is sovereign in His realm, with myriads of angels divided into hierarchies and charged with individual responsibilities. Angels are the administrators of the will of God. Satan imitated God when he arranged his kingdom.

Paul explains that Satan has arranged his realm into different stratas, each with different administrative responsibilities, so that all the forces of hell are arrayed against the child of God. "For we wrestle not against flesh and blood, but against principalities, against powers, against the rulers of the darkness of this world, against spiritual wickedness in high places" (Eph. 6:12).

Through the world Satan executes his purpose. His goal is to dethrone God and enthrone himself as the god of this universe. He seeks to retain all who are presently in his kingdom and prevent them from entering the kingdom of God by a new birth. Satan attempts to reproduce himself in his children so that all the evil and the rebellion and the lawlessness that characterizes him is translated into action.

However, this world system is guilty before God; it has had judgment passed on it. In His holiness God has condemned the character and the conduct of the world. Paul writes, "Now we know that what things soever the law saith, it saith to them who are under the law: that every mouth may be stopped, and all the world may become guilty before God" (Rom. 3:19). On the eve of His crucifixion Jesus looked at the cross and saw a divine judgment on a guilty world. "Now is the judgment of this world: now shall the prince of this world be cast out" (John 12:31). The judgment on this guilty world will be executed in God's own time.

John then gives three reasons why we are forbidden to love the world. First, in verse 15, "If any man love the world, the love of the Father is not in him." A holy God cannot love sin, and if a child of God loves that which God hates, it is never God who is doing the loving through him and in him. Man has no capacity to love with the love of God until he has been born of God and then love, the fruit of the Spirit, is in his life.

In verse 16 John focuses on the content of the world, "All that is in the world, the lust of the flesh, and the lust of the eyes, and the pride of life, is not of the Father, but is of the world." "The lust of the flesh" is the evil inclination of man's sin nature. "The lust of the eyes" refers to Satan tempting the natural man so that evil desire degenerates into lust or covetousness. "The pride of life" is the desire for prominence and adulation.

Satan used these three channels to assault Eve. First, the lust of the flesh, "The woman saw that the tree was good for food" (Gen. 3:6). Further, she saw "that it was pleasant to the eyes," a thing to be coveted. This is the lust of the eye. And it was "a tree desired to make one wise," that is, the pride of life.

Satan also tempted Christ at the outset of His ministry through these three channels. He challenged Christ to make stones into bread — the satisfaction of the flesh. He showed Him the kingdoms of the world — the lust of the eye. He took Him to the pinnacle of the temple and challenged Him to demonstrate His faith — an appeal to the pride of life. Then Satan left Christ because there were no more channels through which to tempt Him.

In verse 17 John gives a third reason for the commandment, "Love not the world." John forbids loving the world because it is transitory. "The world passeth away, and the lust thereof: but he that doeth the will of God abideth for ever."

When Christ comes to earth the second time, among His first official acts will be to bind and remove Satan, casting him into a bottomless pit for the duration of His earthly reign. At the conclusion of that earthly reign, when the Son is ready to turn over the kingdom to the Father, Satan will be loosed and will draw after him those born during the millennial reign who have given only lip service to the King. After that final rebellion, Satan will be cast into the lake of fire forever.

James uses very strong language to warn against befriending the world: "Ye adulterers and adulteresses, know ye not that the friendship of the world is enmity with God? whosoever therefore will be a friend of the world is the enemy of God" (4:4). When we were first redeemed by the blood of Christ, we were brought into a love relationship with the Father and the Son. When one who has been knit to the heart of God loves what God hates, he is committing adultery against God.

Study Questions

1. How is the word *world* used in Scripture?
2. What is John's concept of the world in this letter?
3. What is the believer's relationship to the world?
4. Why is the believer forbidden to love the world?
5. What is the relationship of the world to God?

10

ANTICHRIST HAS COME

1 John 2:18–19

BECAUSE OF THE EVIL OF THE WORLD, Satan's kingdom, John warns against antichrist in verse 18. The word "antichrist" is used in two ways in Scripture. First, it means one who comes as a substitute for Christ. It refers to a person who will appear on the earth in the end time, after the translation of the church into glory. This person will gain worldwide political and religious power that will constitute him as the world's ruler and god. This individual is described in Daniel 7, 8, 11; 2 Thessalonians 2; and Revelation 13, 17, where this person comes as a substitute for Christ. He is a false messiah whom the Lord will judge and destroy at His second advent to this earth.

John also uses the term "antichrist" in the sense of anyone who is opposed to Jesus Christ. John is anticipating the coming of the Antichrist, the lawless rebel who sets himself up as king and god, but he also tells that the antichrist philosophy underlying the coming of this person is already operative in the world. Movements present in John's day opposing Jesus Christ would culminate in the coming of the opposer after the translation of the church into glory. In the meantime, the antichrist philosophy permeates life.

First, antichrist manifests itself in the religious realm. The apostle John is the only New Testament writer who uses the term *antichrist* and each time it refers primarily to the religious realm. After telling that there are many antichrists already operative, he says in 1 John 2:22: ''Who is a liar but he that denieth that Jesus is the Christ? He is antichrist, that denieth the Father and the Son.'' In 4:2–3, ''Every spirit that confesseth that Jesus Christ is come in the flesh is of God; and every spirit that confesseth not that Jesus Christ is come in the flesh is not of God; and this is that spirit of antichrist, whereof ye have heard that it should come, and even now already is it in the world.'' In 2 John 7: ''Many deceivers are entered into the world, who confess not that Jesus Christ is come in the flesh. This is a deceiver and an antichrist.''

John is referring to the doctrine of the person of Jesus Christ. The Word of God clearly teaches that Jesus was born of a virgin in order to clothe His undiminished deity with complete humanity. These two were so inseparably united that the Lord Jesus Christ is God-man—God come in the flesh. All the teaching of the Word of God is based on this doctrine of the person of Jesus Christ.

The philosophy of Satan that permeates this world denies that Jesus Christ is the Son of God come in the flesh, for if one destroys the doctrine of the person of Jesus Christ, he makes the work of Christ of no value.

Antichrist also operates in the political realm. The majority of the earth's peoples are not living under democracy nor do they count democracy a desirable thing. They are living under an atheistic system such as communism or socialism that attempts to offer everything that Jesus Christ will offer to men when He comes back to rule on earth. These worldly political philosophies conflict with a view proclaiming that governments are ordained by God to promote law and order.

The social realm is also affected by antichrist. Young people are growing up in what is commonly called the drug culture. The effect of drugs is to numb the work of the Holy Spirit in convicting men of sin and righteousness and judgment to come. A person either must face his sin and seek the righteousness of Christ so as to escape judgment or deaden the convicting voice of the Holy Spirit. So drugs are offered in opposition to Jesus Christ and as a substitute for Christ's provision for mankind through His death and the new birth.

Antichrist operates in the moral realm. The moralist says man is intrinsically good. All that is needed is to remove the restraints and make a man free and he will express his innate goodness. The moralist also claims there is no absolute standard of right and wrong. Experience determines what is right and wrong. Situation ethics says one can do anything the situation demands. Ignoring the standards of the holiness of God set down in the Word of God, men live like animals and call this acceptable conduct.

Antichrist has also pervaded the arts. The world manifests its opposition to Jesus Christ in art forms such as literature, painting, and music. These forms are not designed to draw men to Christ, but to alienate men from Him. One of Satan's most subtle deceits is the control he exercises over people through modern music. It is not designed to produce peace, harmony, and unity but rather lawlessness, rebellion, and alienation from God. Man cannot use what is basically in opposition to the Lord Jesus Christ for His purposes.

Scripture speaks about our response to antichrist. In 2 Corinthians 6:17 the apostle Paul writes, "Come out from among them, and be ye separate, saith the Lord, and touch not the unclean thing." Anything that partakes of the spirit of this age, manifesting Satan's opposition to Christ is to be totally repudiated. It cannot be followed. We cannot conform to it and expect the blessing of God.

Those who are separate from the world must identify with Jesus Christ. Separation places one in a neutral zone. One who has separated himself from the antichrist system must identify with Jesus Christ if he is to be on the ground of God's blessing and victory. Separation from antichrist must be followed by separation to Jesus Christ.

We who are separated from antichrist and identified with Christ must walk in continuous dependence on the Word of God. Later in this epistle John will explain that we have an anointing from God in the person of the Holy Spirit, who interprets Scripture for us. The Holy Spirit of God also helps the believer to interpret the world so that they understand how all areas of life are permeated by the spirit of antichrist.

Study Questions

1. What does the word *antichrist* mean?
2. How does antichrist manifest itself in the religious realm?
3. What is the test of antichrist doctrine?
4. How does antichrist manifest itself in the social realm?
5. How does antichrist manifest itself in the ethical realm?

11

Defense Against Deception

1 John 2:20–24a

WHEN SATAN ASSAULTS A PERSON he begins by attacking the mind. When he tempted Eve to disobey the command of God, he appealed to her mind, ''Yea, hath God said, Ye shall not eat of every tree of the garden?'' (Gen. 3:1).

In 1 John 2:20–24 the apostle provides the defense against these attacks of Satan. The first defense is found in verse 20. ''Ye have an unction [anointing] from the Holy One, and ye know all things.'' Christ laid the foundation for this truth in His upper room discourse. On the eve of His crucifixion the Lord Jesus told His disciples of the new relationships they would enter with the Father and Son and the Spirit following His ascension. Three times that night the Lord spoke of the coming of the Holy Spirit.

First He promised that the Spirit would come. ''I will pray the Father, and he shall give you another Comforter, that he may abide with you for ever; even the Spirit of truth; whom the world cannot receive, because it seeth him not, neither knoweth him: but ye know him; for he dwelleth with you, and shall be in you'' (John 14:16–17). The Lord Jesus had been their helper. But now He was going away, and so the Lord promised that the Father would send another Person like Himself. ''Comforter'' literally means ''Helper'' or ''the One summoned to one's side to give help.''

In this discourse Jesus is referring specifically to the teaching ministry of the Comforter. "But the Comforter [Helper], which is the Holy Ghost, whom the Father will send in my name, he shall teach you all things, and bring all things to your remembrance, whatsoever I have said unto you" (John 14:26). While the Holy Spirit will help in man's *every* need, the Lord is focusing on one of the paramount needs of the child of God—the need for a teacher who will help him understand Christ's revelation of the Father and of Himself.

For more than three years the Lord had been instructing His disciples, but they had not understood much of His instruction. He had sowed the seed, as it were, and the seed was lying dormant. It did not come to fruit. But the Lord promised that the Spirit would do two things. The Spirit would cause the disciples to recall the very words that Jesus had said, and then He would help them to understand these words and enter into the truth. Christ's teaching is living seed and that seed maintains its life until the showers from heaven bring it to fruit. None of the Lord's teaching was wasted; He had been sowing.

In the same discourse the Lord speaks a third time concerning the ministry of the Comforter.

> When he, the Spirit of truth, is come, he will guide you into all truth: for he shall not speak of himself; but whatsoever he shall hear, that shall he speak: and he will shew you things to come. He shall glorify me: for he shall receive of mine, and shall shew it unto you" (John 16:13–14).

The Spirit's primary ministry is to reveal the things of Christ so that believers enter into intimate fellowship with Him.

After referring to the anointing of the Holy Spirit, John adds, "Ye know all things." John recognized that his spiritual children were once marked by a total inability to understand divine truth but now they have a capacity to understand; they can respond in love to the truth that has been presented. When a man is born again he is given a new mind, the mind of Christ (1 Cor. 2:16). The Holy

Spirit does not try to take the old darkened mind and let the light of the truth of God filter through. In regeneration the Holy Spirit gives us a new mind, a whole new capacity, that can understand and appropriate the truth of God.

John points out in verse 21 that there is an antagonism between truth and error. These are mutually exclusive, and the Holy Spirit never moves in the realm of a lie. "I have not written unto you because ye know not the truth, but because ye know it, and that no lie is of the truth." John is remembering the words of Christ that Satan is a liar and the father of lies (John 8:44). Satan is a liar, not only because he tells lies, but because he deceives men concerning *the truth.* Verses 22 and 23 present Satan's lie, "Who is a liar but he that denieth that Jesus is the Christ? He is antichrist, that denieth the Father and the Son. Whosoever denieth the Son, the same hath not the Father." The Spirit's principal work is to reveal the truth concerning the person of Jesus Christ. The test of any religious system is its response to the question, "Who is Jesus Christ?" The Word of God makes it unequivocably clear that Jesus Christ is the eternal Son of the eternal God, who came in the flesh to save sinners. Satan will never, under any circumstances, permit a man to accept that truth. Satan may concede that God by the spoken word created the universe and that the Bible is the Word of God, but Satan will never concede that Jesus Christ is the Son of God. Every antichrist philosophy at work in the world today must deny that Christ is the Son of God. John says that antichrist, whether it manifests itself in the religious or the political or the moral or the social realm, will be evident through its denial of the person of Jesus Christ. The safeguard against this lie of Satan is the teaching ministry of the Holy Spirit.

There is a second defense against the attacks of Satan, and this moves into the practical realm. In verse 24 John says, "Let that therefore abide in you, which ye have heard from the beginning. If that which ye have heard from the beginning shall remain [abide] in you, ye also shall continue [abide] in the Son, and in the

Father.'' The word *abide* means to get your roots down into
something so that one is being nourished and sustained by that in
which it is rooted. From verse 24 to 27, John is telling God's
children that the truth revealed to them by the Holy Spirit will
preserve them against the lies of Satan. Just as a plant puts roots
down into the ground and is nourished by the soil, so the child of
God puts his roots down into the Word.

On the one hand we have the unceasing ministry of the Holy
Spirit to teach us. On the other hand we have the ministry of the
Word to sustain us. John had no question about the Spirit's teaching ministry. He was concerned about the believer's response to
this ministry of the Spirit. The Spirit would teach the believer
abiding in that instruction, therefore John's teaching of an anointing is coupled with the exhortation to abide in the Spirit's instruction. The believer's relationship to the Word of God, as well
as to the teaching ministry of the Spirit of God, determines to
what degree he can stand against all of Satan's assaults on the
mind.

The writer in Proverbs exhorts: ''Keep thy heart with all dili-
gence; for out of it are the issues of life'' (Prov. 4:23). ''Heart'' is
used to refer to the seat of man's reason. After reminding believers
that they walk in the flesh and are constantly being assaulted by
Satan, Paul sounded the same note as the Old Testament writer
''Casting down [overthrowing] imaginations [the empty processes
of the mind] and every high thing that exalteth itself against the
knowledge of God'' (2 Cor. 10:5). Paul recognizes that the believer is constantly being assaulted by antichrist. He must oppose
and overthrow all these attacks on the mind by ''bringing into
captivity every thought to the obedience of Christ.'' The believer
must hide the Word of God in his mind so that the teachings of
Scripture are ever-present in his thinking.

Study Questions

1. Where do Satan's attacks begin?
2. How does the Holy Spirit safeguard us from Satan's attacks?
3. Why is the Holy Spirit able to be a teacher?
4. Can the Holy Spirit fulfill this ministry to unbelievers?
5. What is the special objective of the Spirit's teaching?

12

WHAT THINK YE OF CHRIST?

1 John 2:24b–29

M**Y WIFE AND** I **FEEL VERY CLOSE** to a family in northern Wisconsin, even though we have only seen them once. We are drawn to them because their son married our daughter. Man, too, is drawn to God through a relationship to His Son. We know the Father because of what we know of the Son

The apostle John emphasizes this great truth in the second chapter of his epistle—we have fellowship with the Father because of the Son. And the privilege of fellowshiping with the Father depends on what we think of His Son, Jesus Christ.

During His earthly ministry Christ had sent the disciples throughout the land of Israel to proclaim His person and work. They announced that in fulfillment of prophecy God had sent His own Son as Savior and Lord. They returned to Christ to report on their ministry.

Christ did not ask how many meetings they had held. He did not want to know the attendance at the services. He asked about the response of the people. "Whom do men say that I the Son of man am?" (Matt. 16:13).

Some of the disciples' listeners had said that Jesus was John the Baptist brought back to life. John had deeply impressed that generation; so it was high praise to be likened to John. Others thought that Elijah had returned to earth to minister again. Elijah had denounced sin in high places and called the people to repentance and warned them of the coming judgment. Some likened Jesus to Jeremiah, the prophet whose heart was broken as he saw the sin of his people inviting the judgment of God. Others could not identify Jesus but recognized that because He came with God's authority He must be one of the prophets. Christ's person and message were more than human phenomena. This was recognized across the land, but no one said that Jesus was the eternal Son of the eternal God become flesh.

Christ then asked, ''Whom say ye that I am?'' Peter, as spokesman for all twelve, confessed the person and work of Christ when he cried out, ''Thou art the [Messiah], the Son of the living God.'' The term *Messiah* embraces the Old Testament prophecy that the Lamb of God would shed His blood to take away the sin of the world before He became the King who rules on earth. He thus confessed to Christ's work. Peter also confessed Christ's person. ''Thou art the Son of the living God.''

After stating the antichrist doctrine in 1 John 2:22–23, the apostle exhorts his children to abide in the truth. The last part of verse 24 explains that if the believer holds to the doctrine of the person and work of Christ, he will abide in the Son and in the Father.

If I think your child is a little monster and you are aware of my opinion, we will not get along together. My attitude toward your child affects your attitude toward me. John says that this is also true of God the Father. If the believer does not think well of the Son, the Father cannot receive him into the warmth of His fellowship because God delights in His Son. He testified from heaven again and again, ''This is my beloved Son, in whom I am well pleased.''

In verse 27 ''anointing'' refers back to verse 20 and the ministry of the Holy Spirit that begins the moment one believes. The teaching ministry of the Spirit interprets the things of Christ for the believer, making it possible for him to fellowship with the Son and through Him with the Father. It is impossible to fellowship with someone you don't know. Fellowship must be based on knowledge. And to make fellowship between the Father and the believer possible, God has sent the Holy Spirit to reveal the things of Christ.

John provides a test to determine what the believer thinks of the Son. "Little children, abide in him; that, when he shall appear, we may have confidence, and not be ashamed before him at his coming. If ye know that he is righteous, ye know that everyone that doeth righteousness is born of him" (vv. 28–29). The believer reveals his estimate of Jesus Christ by the degree to which he reproduces Christ in his life. To know that Jesus Christ was characterized by love and yet not to manifest His love is to think little of Jesus Christ. When one sees the submission of the Lord Jesus to His Father and then rebels, he reveals that he does not think much of Jesus Christ. To see the holiness and righteousness of Jesus Christ as He lived before men and then to walk in unholiness and unrighteousness shows that one does not think much of Jesus Christ. Only when His perfections are reproduced can one say that he thinks well of Jesus Christ.

The important question that John puts forward is not the question, "Can you recognize false doctrine?" His question is, "What think ye of Christ?" What do we think of Him? Do we look at Him through human eyes or through God's eyes? To man He was despised and rejected. Paul had to say in 2 Corinthians 5:16, "Though we have known Christ after the flesh, yet now henceforth know we him no more." Permit the Spirit of God through the Word to reveal the loveliness of the Lord Jesus so that your heart might be drawn to Him and to the Father.

Study Questions

1. What is the final test of any man's doctrine?
2. What is the biblical teaching concerning the person and work of the Messiah?
3. Why does Satan attack this doctrine more than any other?
4. Why does one's doctrine of the person of Christ affect his fellowship with the Father?
5. What are the practical results of a correct doctrine of the person of Christ?

13

WHAT KIND OF LOVE?

1 John 3:1–3

THE THEME OF CHAPTERS ONE AND TWO in John's first epistle is the absolute holiness of God. As John moves into the next section of his epistle, he concentrates on the fact stated in 1 John 4:8: "God is love." Contemplating the love of God, John seems to be overwhelmed at the enormity of it, as though this were a subject far too big to write about or an idea far too great for the mind to comprehend. And so he seems to pause as he says, "Behold, what manner of love the Father hath bestowed upon us" (3:1). The word "behold" is like a flashing light on a highway. It is designed to get someone's attention. It calls one to stop, to ponder, to consider a truth that we might too easily pass by.

When John writes to his disciples, he does not focus on the infinity of the love of God, as Paul had done (Ephesians 3), John emphasizes the quality of God's love. He wants them to comprehend how God loves and what He does for those He loves.

First of all John is emphasizing the unselfishness of the love of God. Natural love is always selfish love. Human love responds to what is attractive, what will satisfy. That love originates externally in what the other person is like and what he does for the first party. Such love must continually be fed to be sustained and worked at to be maintained.

The love of God originates within Himself, because it is God's nature to love. The love of God does not look at a person and ask, "What can you do for Me?" God sees a person's need and devises ways to meet that need.

The love of God, further, is a sacrificial love. This is emphasized in the phrase "bestowed upon us" (v. 1). What John has in mind is seen in verse 16 of this chapter when he said, "Hereby perceive we the love of God, because he laid down his life for us." The measure of the love of God is that God sacrificed His Son. God sent His Son into this world because He loves the world. Jesus Christ was not sent into the world so much for what He could bring out of this world to the Father, but for what He could bring of the Father into this world. It was a sacrificial love that did not count the cost.

John further points out in this verse that the love of God is a separating love. "The world knoweth us not, because it knew him not." The believer has received the love of God and that makes him distinct from the world. The unbeliever talks a great deal about the love of God and the God who is all-loving, but the love of God is known only through the Lord Jesus Christ. The world knows nothing of the love of God in spite of the fact that "God so loved the world, that he gave his only begotten Son, that whosoever believeth in him should not perish, but have everlasting life" (John 3:16).

The world knows of the wrath of God against sin and of the judgment of God against sinners. They recognize the certainty of having to face a just God in a judgment. And when the world sees the believer loved of God and loving God in return, that sends them into a frenzy because they long to be loved. The love of God puts a barrier between the world and the child of God.

In this first verse John also suggests that the love of God is an enriching love. A love "that we should be called the sons [or better, the children] of God." Men are born into this world as the children of the evil one (John 8:44). God in His infinite love regenerated those who had been illegitimately born into another family. He gave them a new birth to bring them into His own family. Children of God is the scriptural concept that God has given His nature to us by a new birth. These children are also called "the sons of God," and sonship in Scripture always emphasizes exalted position and rich inheritance. So the believer can proudly sing,

> A child of the King.
> A child of the King.
> With Jesus my Savior,
> I'm a child of the King.

Then John in verses 2 and 3 emphasizes that the love of God is a conforming love. "We know that when he shall appear, we shall be like him; for we shall see him as he is. And every man that hath this hope in him purifieth himself, even as he is pure." God's love causes the believer to become what God wants him to be. God wants believers to be conformed to the image of His Son, and He has destined that one day they shall be like Christ. It is God's purpose that believers begin to be conformed to Christ in this life, and He loves them into that conformity.

The mystery of the love of God is beyond human comprehension. Paul expressed the magnitude of God's love when he prayed that God would enlarge our understanding, that we might know "what is the breadth, and length, and depth, and height; and to know the love of Christ, which passeth knowledge" (Eph. 3:18–19).

Study Questions
1. How is the love of God demonstrated to men?
2. What is the chief characteristic of the love of God?
3. Show the relationship between love and sacrifice?
4. What does the love of God do for men?
5. What does the love of God produce in a believer?

14

WHAT IS SIN?

1 John 3:4–6

WHEN A SOCIETY DISCUSSES a moral or ethical issue they are raising the basic question, "What is sin?" Unfortunately modern society decides such issues by majority vote; so sin is determined by what is acceptable to society.

The apostle John comes to grips with the issue of sin in verse 4, "Whosoever committeth sin transgresseth also the law: for sin is the transgression of the law." John refers to the Mosaic law, the absolute standard that was revealed to control the conduct of God's children.

The Law was given following God's deliverance of His people out of Egypt. The Israelites had grown up in Egypt and they knew nothing of the true and living God. They knew only the gods of Egypt. Their religious life had been molded by Egyptian society. God gave His law to reveal His character to those whom He had redeemed. Israel was a redeemed people because they had believed God and applied the blood of the Passover lamb, but they did not know Him intimately. The law was given to reveal the character of God and the demands that a holy God made on those who would walk in fellowship with Him.

The apostle John recognizes that any failure to obey the revelation of the character of God must be deemed sin. The law says,

"God does not, therefore you cannot," and "God does, and therefore, you must." The law of God is not intended to deprive men of blessing or enjoyment. It was given to show how God acts, to reveal what God is, so that men might know how to act and how to live. One of the simplest tests as to whether an act is sinful is to ask the question, "Would the Lord Jesus Christ do that?" Anything that is unbecoming to the Lord Jesus Christ must be deemed sinful because it is a violation of the character of God as revealed in the law of God.

In the New Testament a number of ideas are incorporated in the English word "sin." The first idea is a failure to attain, a failure to reach a goal. It applies to a runner who after months of preparation finds himself in the race and he begins to run well. But as he comes to the end of the race, he finds his strength waning and he must drop out of the race.

God's purpose is that His creature be so related to Him that He finds delight in him and the creature delights in the Creator. Man was created to satisfy the heart of God by responding to the Creator. Man is a sinner because he has not reached the purpose that God set before him.

A second word translated "sin" has the idea of missing the mark, missing the target. This suggests a soldier who anxiously awaits the approach of the enemy. As the enemy comes within range, he takes an arrow from his quiver, carefully fits it to the bow, and draws back the bowstring. But the arrow veers off and he misses the mark. Unless an arrow is perfectly straight, the archer cannot find the mark. Scripture emphasizes that because of Adam's sin man is bent, and he will never find the mark. God's purpose was to set a straight path for our feet, but man's foot has turned and he does not reach the mark that God set for him.

A third word translated "sin" has the thought of failing to measure up to a predetermined standard. A young man presented himself to an army recruiter. The recruiter filled out all the papers and then sent him to the medical officer. When the officer measured him, he was an inch short of the minimum requirement. The young man had fallen short of the standard. He was crestfallen, but was determined to reach those standards. He started a program of rigorous stretching exercises, but once again he was rejected because he did not meet the minimum standard.

That is God's concept of sin. The standard by which God measures a man is not other men. God measures men according to the unalterable perfection of His character and work. God's holiness becomes the measuring rod.

Although men are transgressors, John tells how it is possible for them to fellowship intimately with the Father: "Whosoever abideth in him sinneth not" (v. 6).

When we have our roots down into the Lord Jesus Christ so that His life flows through us, we are so conformed to the standards of God's holiness that we can fellowship with Him. Bent arrows can find God's mark. And we who become weary in the race can reach the goal. We who fail to measure up to God's standards can attain the stature of Christ so that God delights in us. The inflexible standards of God are fulfilled as one abides in Jesus Christ. Therefore Paul could write, "To me to live is Christ" (Phil. 1:21).

When John says, "Whosoever sinneth hath not seen him," he is not saying that the one who has been born again can never sin, but rather that the one who is sinning is not experiencing the fullness of the life of Christ. John is not inferring that the one who sins has not been born again, nor that he has lost his salvation. Rather he affirms that when one sins he has left fellowship with God.

Study Questions

1. Why is a correct definition of sin essential to fellowship?
2. How does failure to reach a goal relate to the concept of sin?
3. How does missing the mark relate to the concept of sin?
4. How does failure to measure up relate to the concept of sin?
5. How would you define sin?

15

CHILDREN OF GOD AND CHILDREN OF THE DEVIL

1 John 3:7–10

JOHN'S CONCEPT OF FELLOWSHIP is based on the character of God as stated in 1 John 1:5, "God is light, and in him is no darkness at all." Fellowship with God is possible only as one conforms to the holiness of God. Jesus Christ came to provide us with a righteousness that would make fellowship with God possible.

In 1 John 3:7 John is referring to satanic deception when he says, "Let no man deceive you"—the deception that one can fellowship with God while he is in sin. In verse 6 of this chapter, John has shown us that God and sin are irreconcilable.

In the seventh verse John traces righteousness to its root. Righteous acts come from a righteous nature planted within us, and they are proof of a man's righteousness. "He that doeth righteousness is righteous, even as he [God] is righteous."

The believer possesses two kinds of righteousness; the first is positional righteousness in Christ. Paul wrote: "For he hath made him to be sin for us, who knew no sin; that we might be made the righteousness of God in him" (2 Cor. 5:21).

Scripture makes it clear that we have no righteousness of our own. "All our righteousnesses are as filthy rags" (Isa. 64:6). "Not by works of righteousness which we have done, but according to his mercy he saved us, by the washing of regeneration and the renewing of the Holy Ghost'' (Titus 3:5). Jesus Christ, the Righteous One, assumed our guilt to impart His righteousness to us.

The second aspect of righteousness stressed in the Scriptures is experiential righteousness, our positional righteousness translated into experience. Paul had this in mind in writing to the Philippians,

> This I pray, that your love may abound yet more and more in knowledge and all judgment; that ye may approve things that are excellent; that ye may be sincere and without offence till the day of Christ; being filled with the fruits of righteousness, which are by Jesus Christ, unto the glory and praise of God (1:9–11).

John is stressing that righteous acts result from the righteousness of God given to us. Righteousness is the product of the new nature imparted to us by a new birth.

On the other hand, sin is traced to Satan. ''He that committeth sin is of the devil; for the devil sinneth from the beginning'' (v.8). Sin begins with Satan and works through the fallen nature of men. Satan works through the sin nature of a man, whether born again or not, to produce sin.

John now shows us in verse 8 the purpose of the coming of Christ. ''For this purpose the Son of God was manifested, that he might destroy the works of the devil.'' Christ came to provide sinful men with a new nature, enabling them to live a holy life. He came to make it possible for men to fellowship with a holy God.

While some would teach that the new birth eradicates the old sin nature, it is the teaching of Scripture that the sin nature remains with us until we are translated into God's presence. Paul testifies to the existence of the sin nature in the child of God:

> That which I [old nature] do I [new nature] allow not; for what I [new] would, that do I [old] not; but what I [new] hate, that do I [old]. If then I [old] do that which I [new] would not, I consent unto the law that it is good. Now then it is no more I [new] that do it, but sin [old] that dwelleth in me (Rom. 7:15–17).

Paul is showing that in his experience he recognized two natures operating. The sin nature that he received from his father operated continuously. It was active. It was virulent. Its product was sin. However, Paul recognized that there was a new nature within him imparted by a new birth. This new nature opposed the old, and the product of the new nature was righteousness.

"Whosoever is born of God doth not commit sin" (v. 9). We can read this verse, "That which is born of God doth not commit sin." This refers to the new nature imparted to the child of God at his new birth. Peter refers to this new nature: "That by these ye might be partakers of the divine nature" (2 Peter 1:4). The nature that God imparts cannot commit sin because it is God's nature.

This is what was in John's mind when he said, "For his seed remaineth in him." That is, God's seed, God's nature, abides in God's child and that nature cannot sin because it is born of God. We therefore could paraphrase verse 4 this way, "That which has been born of God does not commit a single sin, for it is God's nature that has been planted in him, and this nature cannot sin because it is born of God." Thus John is not saying that sin is impossible in the life of the child of God. He traces sin in the life of the child of God to its root—the old fallen nature. God's children do sin. That is why John wrote, "If we [believers] confess our sins, he is faithful and just to forgive us our sins, and to cleanse us from all unrighteousness" (1 John 1:9).

John closes this part of his message by giving us a test of sonship. "In this the children of God are manifest, and the children of the devil: whosoever doeth not righteousness is not of God, neither he that loveth not his brother."

There are two tests that one is a child of God. First, he will do righteousness. The unsaved man has no capacity to do righteousness. He may do things that are good in the sight of men, but he cannot act righteously. The only one who can do righteousness acceptable to God is the one who has had the righteousness of God imputed to him. Righteousness is God's work in a man. No man can produce righteousness himself. But when God has imputed righteousness to a man, He can then work through that new nature to produce righteousness acceptable to Himself. The unsaved man does not have righteousness and therefore God does not work through him to produce works of righteousness. John therefore affirms that the first proof that one is a child of God is that the works of God are seen in his life.

The second proof is that the love of God will be produced through God's child. The sinful man is essentially selfish. Therefore he cannot love with the unselfish love of God. Unselfish love is proof that God is at work in a man's life. Therefore love for the brother becomes a proof of fellowship.

Our fellowship with God, then, does not depend on the eradication of the sin nature. We fellowship with God as we walk in the light of His holiness and as we fellowship one with another.

Study Questions

1. What is the root of sin in the believer's life?
2. What is the root of righteousness in the believer's life?
3. What is imputed righteousness?
4. What is the relationship of imputed righteousness to righteousness in daily life?

16

GOD'S COMMAND TO LOVE

1 John 3:11–15

WE TEND TO BELIEVE that in this age of grace there are no commandments for which the child of God is responsible. Nothing could be further from the truth. The commandments of Jesus are as binding on us as the commandments given to Moses in the Old Testament. We are dealing with one of those commandments when John writes, "This is the message that ye heard from the beginning, that we should love one another." "Love one another" is not an exhortation, it is a commandment. And the one who does not love as God has loved him is a lawbreaker. No violator of God's commandments can enjoy fellowship with the Father and the Son.

This was not a new commandment John was introducing to his readers. From the opening pages of the Old Testament this commandment had been in force. While some would interpret the phrase "from the beginning" as referring to the beginning of Christ's new revelation while here on earth, it seems best to take this back to the very beginning of divine revelation.

The Pharisees were preoccupied with the Mosaic law. Realizing that a true Israelite was expected to obey the law, they sought to clarify the law by reducing it to the minimum. They had codified the law into 365 prohibitions and 250 commandments.

However, it became evident to them that it was impossible for a man to keep all of these so they tried to arrange the commandments in order of importance. Their inability to conclude which commandment took precedence over the other demonstrates that the law is a unit.

So one of the lawyers of the Pharisees came to Christ to ask a question (Matt. 22:35–40). He was not seeking information; he wanted to embarrass Christ. He asked what seemed to be an unanswerable question. Christ had said that He had come to fulfill the law. If He is to fulfill the law, He must understand the spirit of the law as well as the letter. So the Pharisee asked Jesus, "What is the great commandment in the law? Which commandment takes precedence? Which law is it most important that we observe?"

Without hesitating the Lord answered, "Thou shalt love the Lord thy God with all thy heart, and with all thy soul, and with all thy mind. This is the first and great commandment." This commandment takes precedence over all others. "The second is like unto it, Thou shalt love thy neighbor as thyself. On these two commandments hang all the law and the prophets."

The law of God was written on two tablets of stone. The first tablet contained commandments that govern man's responsibility to God. The second tablet presented commandments and prohibitions that govern man's relationship to men. The only way a man ever can obey the first part of the law is that his love for God takes precedence over all else. When he is totally occupied with God he will not be occupied with lesser things.

If a man is preoccupied with the good of his neighbor he will not do evil to him, so obedience to the second tablet of the law must be founded on love for one's neighbor. Love for one's neighbor is the outgrowth of love for God. Love for God takes precedence over all else and produces love in the family of God and love that extends beyond to those whom God loves. Thus the Lord was able to meet this challenge by showing that from the beginning love for God and the consequent love for those who are our neighbors was what God required of men.

Jesus gave the same commandment to the disciples in the upper room. "This is my commandment, that ye love one another, as I have loved you. Greater love hath no man than this, that a man lay down his life for his friends. Ye are my friends, if ye do whatsoever I command you" (John 15:12–14). The Lord is emphasizing the connection between love and obedience. Love for God produces obedience. The way to please God is to have a heart that is set on Him. And a heart that is set on Him obeys His commands. Obedience manifests itself when we love others.

A person who knows the command of God but who does not obey is viewed by God as a lawbreaker and no lawbreaker can have fellowship with a holy God. John in the verses that immediately preceded has defined sin as any violation of the law of God. He has revealed to us the fact that Jesus Christ was no lawbreaker. He was perfectly obedient to the Word of God. So the fellowship that the Son enjoyed with the Father was possible because of His perfect obedience. The consequence of this teaching is that the only way we can enjoy fellowship with the Father is to obey His commandments. And which is the greatest commandment? "Love one another."

After stating the command in verse 11, John commands them not to love "as Cain, who was of that wicked one, and slew his brother. And wherefore slew he him? Because his own works were evil, and his brother's righteous" (v. 12). In Genesis 4 we have the record of the birth of two sons to Adam and Eve. Cain, the firstborn, was a tiller of the soil. Abel, the second, was a keeper of the sheep. Both Cain and Abel received the same revelation concerning access to God. When Adam sinned, God became priest, sacrificing an animal and covering Adam's sin with the blood of that animal and covered his nakedness with the skin. That was a revelation of how to approach God.

Later these two brothers offered sacrifices to God. Cain acted in disobedience because of the evil of his heart. Abel acted in obedience because of the righteousness of his heart. When Cain saw that his offering was rejected and his brother's accepted, he murdered his brother. This murder is one of the most heinous crimes recorded in the Word of God. The only crime that could perhaps take precedence was the crime of Judas. Why is this murder such a heinous crime? Because Cain not only killed, he also hated his brother. His sin was a sin against love.

John teaches the importance of obeying the commandment of God, "Love one another." by saying that believers may like Cain manifest hatred that springs from an evil heart and be guilty of Cain's sin. It was not murder that made Cain's heart evil; the evil produced the murder. Cain's heart was evil because it was not controlled by love. And John is concerned lest an evil heart should manifest itself in the family of God and that the love commanded should not be demonstrated and the family consequently be destroyed.

In verses 13–15 John recognizes that one will not see this love manifested in the world. Therefore one cannot pattern his conduct after the world, for the world hates. It is only the believer who has the capacity to demonstrate the unselfish love of God, to consider not himself, but the other person. The love of God is characterized by its pure unselfishness. His love does not consider what the other person can do for the one loving, it is concerned about what the one loving can do for the other person. The world is characterized by hatred, and if a believer patterns his conduct after the life of the world, he will never enjoy fellowship with the Father and the Son. Christ's joy in the Father came from His love for the Father producing perfect obedience. So John says, "We know that we have passed from death unto life, because we love the brethren." If there is love in the heart for a brother in Christ, it is evident that we have been born into God's family, and have been given God's capacity to love, because the world does not have that capacity and will never manifest affection.

John causes us to examine ourselves when he says, "He that loveth not his brother abideth in death. Whosoever hateth his brother is a murderer: and ye know that no murderer hath eternal life abiding in him" (vv. 14–15). John is not saying that a saved man cannot hate. He is not saying even that a saved man cannot kill, because he can and does. What John is saying is that no man who is controlled by the new life of Christ can hate. No man who is under the control of the love of God can manifest hatred in murder. One can be saved and hate, but one cannot be living by the power of the new life of Christ and hate at the same time. We can be alive and still live in the realm of death.

The man who does not love his brother is being controlled by death. He is being controlled by that old sin nature within him. He is not being controlled by the new life of Christ because the characteristic of Christ's life is love that produces obedience to the commands of God. John is emphasizing this truth because his aim in this epistle is to introduce believers to the joy of intimate fellowship with the Father and the Son. He wants the same radiant joy that characterized the Lord Jesus during His earthly life to characterize them.

So he points out that the Lord Jesus, when He was among them, loved the Father and showed His love for the Father by perfect obedience to the Father because love always begets obedience. If they are to enter into that fullness of joy that Christ had, they must love the Father, manifest that love in obedience to the Father in keeping His commandments, the first commandment being that we love the family of God. John has made it very clear that divisions and anger, strife, maliciousness, gossip, and backbiting among believers take one out of the will of God and put him in the class of a lawbreaker. We have violated the command of God to "Love one another." This makes fellowship with God impossible.

Study Questions

1. How can there be commandments in the New Testament?
2. What is the relation of love to law?
3. Why does John make reference to Cain?
4. Why is love a proof of salvation?
5. How does hate affect fellowship?

17

WHAT LOVE DEMANDS

1 John 3:16–18

SO UNFATHOMABLE IS THE LOVE OF CHRIST, Paul prays that the Ephesians "comprehend . . . what is the breadth, and length, and depth, and height; and to know the love of Christ, which passeth knowledge" (3:18–19). We will never find the love of Christ by looking at the world around us, for the world knows nothing of this love. The apostle John has reaffirmed Jesus' command in the upper room, "Love one another." The commandment of God is that the child of God love as God loves. We do not wear the badge of relationship to Jesus Christ until that love is manifested. John now explains the love of God so that his readers can love one another. "Hereby perceive we the love of God, because he laid down his life for us." In this sacrifice we perceive the love of God.

Frequently in Scripture a writer will refer to one of the saints for the purpose of illustration. When Paul wanted to teach the truth of justification by faith, he appealed to the life of Abraham. As Abraham believed God, so are we to believe God. Many of the Christian virtues can be illustrated by the lives of the saints. But when John would illustrate the love of Christ, he must appeal to God Himself, for the world does not know the love of Christ, nor does it satisfy God's command, "Love one another." So John refers to God the Father.

It was not sufficient for God merely to announce His love to man. It became necessary for God to translate His love into action. The incarnation of Jesus Christ was God veiling the glory of heaven in human flesh and sending His Son into the world. His coming into the world through the virgin birth was an evidence of God's love for sinful men. God met man's need; the love God reproduced in the child of God responds to the needs of others.

"Whoso hath this world's good, and seeth his brother have need, and shutteth up his bowels of compassion from him, how dwelleth the love of God in him?" (v. 17) is an interpretation and application of verse 16. God in His wisdom provided for man's need by offering salvation. John wants us to realize that the love of God reproduced in us will recognize the need of others. An individual first sees the need, and then he recognizes he has the ability to meet that need. The love of God is not only an emotional response such as mercy or pity. The love of God will give rise to such emotions, but we have not loved with the love of God until we act.

We ask, "But whom am I to love?" John is writing about love in the family of God. We are responsible to love the members of the family of God—the family of God with whom we are closely associated. But if we stop here we are little better than the lawyer who came to test Christ. He was a scholar of Mosaic law and its interpretation. He tested Jesus by asking, "What shall I do to inherit eternal life?" What laws must I keep to have eternal life? Our Lord responded, "What is written in the law?" The lawyer replied, using the same response the Lord had given when He was asked this question on another occasion. The lawyer said, "Thou shalt love the Lord thy God with all thy heart, and with all thy soul, and with all thy strength, and with all thy mind; and thy neighbour as thyself" (Luke 10:27). Love for God means total commitment to God and love for one's neighbor demands obedience to the law of God in fulfilling every social relationship. So love is the fulfillment of the law.

After the lawyer summarized the law he stood convicted of his own unworthiness. His excuse was to plead ignorance. "He, willing to justify himself, said unto Jesus, and who is my neighbour?"

Jesus then told the familiar story of the man traveling down from Jerusalem to Jericho. As he was going through the wilderness of Judea among mountain recesses, he was attacked by thieves. The thieves stripped him and wounded him. He was lying alongside the road, obviously in need. A priest walked by, and he recognized the man's need. The priest had the means to meet that need, but he had no compassion. A little later a Levite passed by. He recognized the need and could have met the man's need. But he too had no compassion.

Later a Samaritan, people despised by the Jews, came by. He responded to the need. First he bound up the man's wounds, using oil to soothe and wine to purify. He brought him to an inn, and cared for him. He even provided for the man's future needs.

The Lord asked the lawyer, "Which now of these three, thinkest thou, was neighbour unto him that fell among the thieves?" And he said, "He that shewed mercy on him." So our Lord's definition of our neighbor is, "Any man in need, whose need you are able to meet."

To know the need but have no capacity to meet it does not put me under obligation. Nor am I responsible if I am ignorant of the need. But where there is knowledge, coupled with ability, I have a responsibility to manifest the love of Christ to one in need.

This is a very pointed lesson; it removes the boundaries from our narrow concepts of our responsibility. Our responsibility becomes as wide as the love of God.

John gives a word of caution: our affection must not be in words alone, words must be accompanied by deeds. He does not say, "Don't tell anybody you love them." He is saying, "Don't let words be your only communication."

Perhaps three of the hardest words to say are, "I love you."

This is not in reference to husband and wife, or children and parents, although many may suffer from a difficulty to verbalize our deepest emotions even to those dearest to us. This refers to the family of God, the body of Christ. There is social pressure against saying to another adult, "I love you."

The world knows nothing about this kind of love. It has such a distorted concept of love that a man is suspect if he says to a woman, "I love you." Should a man say to another man, "I love you," he is accused of perversion. When a child of God expresses love in the presence of a worldling, he is apt to be misunderstood. So we are fearful.

We also suffer because we fail to respond to those in need. People are often surprised by the love shown to them by members of their church. But isn't it unfortunate that someone has to be helpless or in desperate need before we show affection?

To smother love or to leave it unexpressed is to frustrate the work of the Spirit. We must learn to express our love for one another. Love does not ask, "What can you do for me?" Love asks, "What can I do for you?" Love asks not so much, "How are you today?" but "What can I do for you today?"

Whom am I responsible to love? Any man in need. There is not one of us who does not need to be loved. We have the responsibility to show the love of Christ by meeting one another's need.

Study Questions

1. How did God prove His love for the world?
2. How do believers prove their love for believers?
3. What is John's concept of love?
4. How does the parable of the Good Samaritan define a neighbor?
5. Contrast God's love with the world's love.

18

A CONDEMNED HEART

1 John 3:19–24

THE FIRST EPISTLE OF JOHN is strongly influenced by Jesus' state-
ment to the disciples in John 13:34: "A new commandment I give
unto you, That ye love one another; as I have loved you, that ye
also love one another." Jesus had demonstrated this love earlier by
taking the role of a servant and washing their feet. Christ's love
eventually led Him to Calvary. In order to lead his spiritual
children into a life of intimate fellowship with the Father John
teaches they must love one another.

In 1 John 3:19–24 the apostle deals with the problem of a heart
that condemns itself. While we know the love of God, we do not
fully manifest it. We do not love as He loved. John writes consola-
tion and instruction to help us cope with this problem.

He tells us that a believer's love for others is confirmation of
sound doctrine. "Hereby we know that we are of the truth, and
shall assure our hearts before Him" (v. 19). The apostles wanted
believers to stand firm in the truth. The body of truth revealed to
the apostles by the Spirit was called "The Faith" or "The Truth."
Paul therefore charges Timothy to hold "faith, and a good conscience; which some having put away concerning faith [The Faith]
have made shipwreck" (1 Tim. 1:19).

False doctrine will manifest itself in evil practice, but true doctrine will produce obedience to God's commands. If you examine a bush in your yard and find a tender green bud, you know it has survived the winter. The roots must be alive because a bud has appeared. In the same way, love for others reveals that we hold to sound doctrine.

In verses 20–21 John shows us that love for one another assures us of our relationship to the Father. He deals with the negative aspect first. "If our heart condemn us, God is greater than our heart, and knoweth all things." John recognizes that believers will have to say, "I know I do not love as Christ loved." The love of Christ does manifest itself in us, but that is not our outstanding characteristic. There are times when love is not present, and this causes doubt. If one gauges his relationship to the Father by emotions and experience, he would have no assurance of his relationship to God. While we judge our relationship to God by experience, John instructs us to determine this relationship by faith. God knows that we have faith in Him. If our hearts condemn us and question whether we are related to Jesus Christ, God is satisfied because He judges on the basis of faith.

There is, tragically, a theological wave engulfing the church that determines doctrine not by the Word of God, but by personal experience. Practices contrary to Scripture are being advocated. When confronted with the Word of God, multitudes say, "I don't care what it says, my experience tells me different." They are basing their relationship to God on sinful human experience, and consequently such a person is insecure.

In verse 21 John says, "Beloved, if our heart condemn us not, then have we confidence toward God." If our heart does not convict us of breaking God's love commandment, this means we are in fact loving others, and this assures us.

When Paul lists the fruit of the Spirit in Galatians 5, he mentions love first. Why? Because we are commanded to love. Obedience to this commandment is like the life of the root manifesting itself on the branch.

John explains in verses 22–23 that obedience to Christ's love commandment is the basis for answered prayer. "Whatsoever we ask, we receive of him, because we keep his commandments, and do those things that are pleasing in his sight" (v.22). Loving one another is a prerequisite to answered prayer. We have the right to pray because we are related to Jesus Christ by faith, but that relationship does not guarantee that our prayers will be answered. Not until we have obeyed Christ's commandment will our prayers be answered. On the other hand, if we do not keep His commandments our prayers will not be answered.

In verse 23 John tells us there are two commandments. First, "Believe on the name of his Son Jesus Christ." Faith in Jesus Christ establishes relationship with the Father and is the foundation of prayer. The second commandment is as essential as the first: "Love one another, as he gave us commandment." John is offering a lesson that Jesus had taught his disciples on a number of occasions. If a child of God is out of fellowship with another believer, he is out of fellowship with the Father. When the right relationship does not exist between children in a family, the relationship between the father and children will also be strained. Prayer will be hindered if family members are out of fellowship, just as they are when we are out of fellowship with a brother or sister in Christ.

The command to love is as much an imperative as the command to believe. The necessity of faith is obvious. The necessity to love ought to be equally obvious. The Lord made this clear in Matthew 5. He is speaking to Jews, who worshiped and prayed in a form that differs from ours, but the lesson is pertinent nonetheless. "If thou bring thy gift to the altar, and there rememberest that thy brother hath aught against thee; leave there thy gift before the altar, and go thy way; first be reconciled to thy brother, and then come and offer thy gift" (Matt. 5:23–24). Then Jesus adds this word, "Agree with thine adversary quickly, whiles thou art in the way with him; lest at any time the adversary deliver thee to the judge, and the

judge deliver thee to the officer, and thou be cast into prison.''
We conclude from the warning about being thrown into prison
that the offence the Lord has in mind is a failure to discharge a
financial obligation to our brother. The brother who is coming to
worship and pray is in debt to a brother, but has failed to meet that
obligation. The creditor has the right to accuse him before a judge
and have him thrown into a debtor's prison. Jesus says that the
door to the holiest is closed, not because God is not gracious nor
because He cannot hear, but because this man was alienated from
his brother.

As important as it is for you to worship and pray, it is more
important to be reconciled with your brother. Do not go to God
until you have straightened out matters with your brother. What
could be clearer? Disruption of fellowship with a brother, for any
cause, disrupts fellowship with God. One is rightly related to Jesus
Christ by faith because he has obeyed the first commandment, and
he is able to pray to God because he has obeyed the second. Love is
the basis of answered prayer.

Finally, John points out in verse 24 that obedience to this
commandment to love as Christ loved is the basis of our fellowship
with the Father. ''He that keepeth his commandments dwelleth
[abides] in him.'' In 1:3 John has told us he was writing to
introduce his readers to the glorious truth of fellowship with the
Father and with His Son. There is no real satisfaction for the child
of God apart from intimate fellowship with the Father. ''And these
things write we unto you, that your joy may be full'' (v. 4). But
there can be no fellowship with the Father apart from fellowship
with the saints. The believer who keeps God's commandments of
faith in God and love for one another abides in fellowship with
Him.

Study Questions

1. What is the source of condemnation in the believer's heart?
2. What is the relationship of love and truth?
3. What is the believer's assurance if love is absent in his life?
4. What is the relationship of love and answered prayer?
5. Show from Matthew 5:23–25 how this principle operates.

19

TESTING THE TEACHER

1 John 4:1–6

WHILE JOHN DOES SPEAK of loving one another, he also wants to safeguard God's children against prostituting their affections. An indiscriminate love will violate the commandment to love as Christ loved. Therefore John writes, "Beloved, believe not every spirit, but try [test] the spirits whether they are of God: because many false prophets are gone out into the world" (v. 1).

When John refers to "spirit," he is not speaking of a being that comes from the demonic world. He is referring to a teacher or prophet.

The preaching arrangement in the early church is the background of John's injunction here. They knew little of a formal arrangement where the assembly of believers had a pastor who taught the Word of God. Like apostles, the teachers itinerated from church to church. They depended on hospitality being extended to them when they came to teach.

We read in Hebrews 13:1–2, "Let brotherly love continue. Be not forgetful to entertain strangers: for thereby some have entertained angels [God's emissaries] unawares." The obligation to love included extending hospitality, particularly to those whom God had sent to minister the Word of God.

We can well imagine a knock on the door and the householder

opening the door to a man who would identify himself as one sent
by God with His message. The householder would remember
John's command to show hospitality as a sign of love, and so he
would be tempted to invite the visitor in. But John cautioned them
that there are both true and false teachers. It is necessary to
discriminate between the two. Therefore the warning is given to
safeguard the commandment to love one another. One must use
discrimination in his affection.

John begins by pointing out that there are two kinds of teachers:
those who come with the truth and those who deny the truth and
come with error. But as we move on in the passage John draws a
distinction between the origin of the false teachers and the origin of
the true teachers. In verse 3 he says, "Every spirit that confesseth
not that Jesus Christ is come in the flesh is not of God: and this is
that spirit of antichrist, whereof ye have heard that it should come,
and even now already is it in the world." Again in verse 5, "They
are of the world: therefore speak they of the world, and the world
heareth them." The false teachers originate from the world.

Earlier in the study of this epistle we have seen that the world is
an organized system under the headship of Satan. In order to attain
his goal of dethroning God and enthroning himself, Satan sends
out representatives to teach. They teach the thinking of this world,
the thinking of Satan, and they get a response because they are
saying what the worldling wants to hear.

In contrast, there are those who are of God (v. 4). And again,
"We are of God: he that knoweth God heareth us; he that is not of
God heareth not us. Hereby know we the spirit of truth, and the
spirit of error" (v. 6).

The true teacher comes by divine authority. His authority is in
the truth, and the Spirit of God testifies to the truth. When the man
of God speaks to God's children, the Spirit of God confirms the
truth to the listeners.

In 1 John 2:20 John said, "Ye have an unction [anointing] from
the Holy One, and ye know all things." The child of God who

listens with the ear of the Spirit of God will not be deceived by error, because the Spirit will never approve the deception of a false teacher.

John now considers the two doctrines promulgated by these two teachers. First he deals with the true doctrine. In verse 2, "Every spirit that confesseth that Jesus Christ is come in the flesh is of God." Again in verse 4, "Greater is he that is in you, than he that is in the world." The Word of God is the test of the doctrine of any teacher.

This is clearly illustrated in the Old Testament when, after God had revealed the law through Moses, He reveals how to detect a false prophet. "If there arise among you a prophet, or a dreamer of dreams, and giveth thee a sign or a wonder, and the sign or the wonder come to pass, whereof he spake unto thee, saying, Let us go after other gods, which thou hast not known, and let us serve them" (Deut. 13:1–2). Here is a prophet who appears before the people of God claiming to be God's spokesman. He performs miracles and predicts the future. Looking at his prediction and at the wonders that he did one would say, "This man must come by the power of God. We must listen to what he says." But in spite of the signs, and visions, and predictions, God demands:

> Thou shalt not hearken unto the words of that prophet, or that dreamer of dreams: for the LORD your God proveth you, to know whether you love the LORD your God with all your heart and with all your soul. Ye shall walk after the LORD your God, and fear him, and keep his commandments, and obey his voice, and ye shall serve him, and cleave unto him. And that prophet, or that dreamer of dreams, shall be put to death (Deut. 13:3–5).

Such a man may seem to have the credentials to prove that he has come from God, but God said that if his word was contrary to the Word of God, he was to be put to death. The evidence of the truth of the prophet was in the word that he spoke. Does it conform to the Word of God? If it does not, he is a false prophet.

God is zealous to preserve His Word because it is our access to Him. When a false prophet changes that Word he has closed the door that God has opened.

John gives us a specific test by which we determine whether a man is a man of God or a false teacher. The test is in verse 2, "Every spirit that confesseth that Jesus Christ is come in the flesh is of God."

In the first chapter of his Gospel John had outlined the doctrine of the person of Christ: Christ is the eternal Son of the eternal God; He is equal with God; He is the Creator; He is the One who reveals the Father to us; He is life; He is the Savior. Now John can write and say, "The test of any teacher is what he thinks about the person of Jesus Christ." If a man denies the truth about the person of Jesus Christ, he is a false teacher. He does not come from God. He is an emissary of Satan, no matter how much he professes to be God's spokesman. Without exception false teachers deny that Jesus Christ is the eternal Son of the eternal God, who by His substitutionary death on the cross provided us with eternal salvation.

In 2 John 10, John says, "If there come any unto you, and bring not this doctrine, receive him not into your house, neither bid him God speed." If we extend hospitality without discriminating we are violating the principle of love. If one professes to come with God's message, and, without testing him, we expose the saints to his false teaching, we are his partner in deception. And if we send him on his way with our blessing (that is, material support), then we are convicted by the Word: "For he that biddeth him God speed is partaker of his evil deeds" (2 John 11).

In the apostle's day the Word had to be communicated person to person. With the many means of communication today we can invite all kinds of false teachers into our homes without being in the presence of another person. Whether a man comes in person to propagate his doctrine, or whether he does it by some other means, if we invite him into our home we have become a partaker of his evil deeds.

We have no right to accept any word that purports to come from God without testing it by the Word of God. God commands us to love. But he safeguards that by commanding us to be discriminating in our love. Test the teachers by the Word of God. Test them by their doctrine of the person and the work of Jesus Christ, for multitudes of false teachers have come to propagate Satan's doctrine. We must test the spirits, lest we fall into the deception of the evil one.

Study Questions

1. Why is it necessary to test teachers?
2. Why did the command to love need a safeguard?
3. What is the test of a teacher?
4. What is the source of the false doctrine of the false teacher?
5. How should a believer respond to a false teacher?

20

GOD SENT HIS SON

1 John 4:7–11

THE LOVE OF GOD IN CHRIST had so captivated the apostle John that it became the central theme of his ministry. The critic sees this note woven like a golden thread throughout this epistle and concludes that it is the rambling of a senile mind. But how the heart of the child of God leaps in response to the love that John showed for the Lord and for the saints. Far from being the musings of a senile man, this epistle throbs with the heartbeat of God.

In verses 9 and 10 John emphasizes that the love of God was demonstrated by sending Christ: "In this was manifested the love of God toward us, because that God sent his only begotten Son into the world. . . ." God clothed Himself with flesh and stepped out of heaven into this world and lived a life so that men could become intimately knowledgeable about God. It was not necessary for God to reveal Himself to His creation. Since man and God are separated by the guilt of sin, God did not have to come into this world to reveal Himself, but He chose to do so. Why? Because God is love. God wanted to reveal Himself and His love toward men who were separated from Him.

God also manifested His love through the death of His Son. God's love for the Son was eternal and unchangeable, but God gave His Son up to death. The measure of the love of God is not so much a measure of the distance from heaven to earth as it is a measure of the distance from the throne to the cross, for it is there that men see the greatness of the love of God.

When the Son of God came into the world, there was no separation between the Father and the Son, for they continued to enjoy intimate communion. But when the Son went to the cross, He was separated from the Father by death. And in that separation we have a revelation of the love of God.

The apostle tells us the Son came into the world "that we might live through Him." God actually gives of Himself to those who put their faith in Jesus Christ and put themselves under His atoning death. God takes those who were enemies and dead in sin, and gives them life and brings them into His own family as His well-beloved children.

The world stands in amazement when a family takes a retarded or deformed child into their home and loves the child as if it were their own. How much greater was the love of God that looked on us in our deformity of sin and took us into His family and made us His heirs.

To climax this survey of the love of God, the apostle says in verse 10, "Herein is love, not that we loved God, but that he loved us, and sent his Son to be the propitiation for our sins." John is referring to the value of the death of Christ and the great work that God accomplished for sinners on the cross so that we might become members of God's family. *Propitiation* is one of the most beautiful words in the Word of God. In Leviticus 16 we find in one of Israel's annual rituals a foreshadowing of Christ as our propitiation. There Moses instructed Israel concerning the Day of Atonement. That day begins with the recognition that men are separated from God and have in themselves no approach to God. God took up residence between the cherubim above the mercy seat on the ark of the covenant. Not even Aaron could come into the presence of God on his own merit because men are sinners and God is holy. Aaron was commanded to kill a goat, which provided access into the presence of God. The blood of the sacrifice was to be placed on the mercy seat.

The writer to the Hebrews shows that Jesus Christ has fulfilled this Old Testament ritual. In Hebrews 9 we discover that God is unapproachable, but that Jesus Christ offered His blood as a sacrifice to God. "How much more shall the blood of Christ, who through the eternal Spirit offered himself without spot to God, purge your conscience from dead works to serve the living God?" (9:14).

The New Testament writers tell us that because of sin God is unapproachable. But Jesus Christ has come and taken our sins in His own body. He has covered those sins with His own blood and offered Himself as a sacrifice to God. Now God can approach man and throw the door open wide to His presence.

Jesus Christ is the One who satisfies God. The blood of Christ is the basis on which God is satisfied; so God can now stretch out His hands to sinners. The death of Jesus Christ did not change the heart of God, as if One who hated us now loves us, rather it opened the floodgate so that the love of God for sinners could be poured out to them through Jesus Christ. This is what John has in mind when he speaks of "propitiation."

Love for God never originates in the heart of man. Love originates in the heart of God and kindles a love for God in the heart of God's enemies. That is what John is emphasizing in verse 10 when he said, "Not that we loved God," God's love for sinners brings them into the full experience of His love and into full partnership in His life.

"Let us love one another" (vv. 7,11) emphasizes an added facet of the truth John taught in chapter 3. Earlier, love for the brethren referred to physical and material needs. In chapter 4, John presents an entirely different concept—spiritual needs. We ought to share spiritual blessings with others to bring them into the love of Christ and the life of Christ.

This was the nature of Christ's ministry. He continually was meeting the physical needs of men. He fed the hungry. He healed the sick. He raised the dead. But our Lord was far more involved in meeting spiritual needs.

Our Lord chose a few men. He could have ministered to multiplied thousands every time He chose to teach. But our Lord left the multitudes and withdrew to minister to a handful of men. Scripture does not belabor what He did for them physically, nor how He provided for them materially. But it does tell us how He invested His life in these men and taught them the truth of God, and revealed the love of God, and prepared them for a ministry of the Word of God.

Christ was in the business of making disciples. He made disciples by dealing with men individually. The burden of the heart of the apostle John in this particular passage is that his children, who have recognized an obligation to minister to one another materially, should occupy themselves in a spiritual ministry to one another. He desired that these saints seek out another individual with whom they might share the love of Christ and the life of Christ and build into the life of that individual what Christ had built into them. Christ made disciples. Now John wants his spiritual children to become men who make disciples.

We measure our ministry by the number to whom we minister. A Sunday school teacher counts the size of his class. The pastor pays attention to the size of the congregation. God does not evaluate by numbers, but by results. Results do not necessarily come by ministering to multitudes, but by building into the life of the individual.

In our relationships we begin with friendship. People become friends because of some mutual interest such as a hobby or business. And then friendship ought to progress to fellowship, which is friendship that takes on the added dimension of the Lord Jesus Christ. Fellowship, in turn, lays the foundation for discipleship, which is the process of helping a fellow believer to mature in Christ. A congregation may mature by sitting together under the ministry of the Word of God, but a congregation will multiply when each individual disciples another.

If you have thought you discharged your responsibility to the obligation of love by looking after the material needs of some saint, then let God open your vision so that to these material concerns should be added another concern: to share the love of Christ and the life of Christ by making a disciple for the Lord Jesus. The love of God demands it, and we do not fulfill our obligation to His love until we do it.

Study Questions

1. Where does love originate?
2. How can love be discerned?
3. How did Christ become a propitiation for sinners?
4. How does the manifestation of love in 1 John 4 differ from that of chapter 3?
5. How can we minister to spiritual needs?

21

THE SAVIOR OF THE WORLD

1 John 4:12 –15

GOD'S LOVE IS A SELFLESS LOVE. It considers only the welfare of those whom He loves. If God considered Himself, He would not have sent the Lord Jesus Christ into the world.

Why should an innocent man die? The apostle John gives us the answer. "And we have seen and do testify that the Father sent the Son to be the Saviour of the world" (v. 14). There is perhaps no more tender name given to Jesus than "Savior." He is the Lord Jesus Christ. He is the Son of God. He is the Son of man. He is the Servant of Jehovah. He is David's greater Son. But above all, He is the Savior.

The Word of God clearly reveals to us the bondage from which we have been delivered by our Savior. First of all, because we were sinners, we were in bondage to Satan. We needed to be delivered from Satan's dominion. When Adam disobeyed God, he consciously submitted to the authority of Satan. He became a bondslave of Satan. Man had no power to loose the shackles of Satan and deliver himself. And this necessitated a Deliverer who could reach us in our bondage to Satan and proclaim liberty to the captives.

Paul writes: "Who [Jesus Christ] hath delivered us from the power of darkness, and hath translated us into the kingdom of his dear Son'' (Col. 1:13). He has delivered us from the dominion of Satan and brought us into His kingdom, where He rules as Sovereign.

The Lord Jesus also came to save men from bondage to the law. The law was a taskmaster, a ruler over slaves. The law passed judgment on men because they violated the holy standards of God revealed in the law. Men were in bondage to the law of conscience. Paul said in Romans 2:15 that the conscience is the law of God written into the heart of every man, revealing the demands of God and accusing the individual of violating God's holiness.

The revelation given to Israel through Moses was another taskmaster that held men in bondage. The law revealed the demands of the holiness of God, and it passed a sentence of death on all who did not measure up to these standards. Men were born in bondage to the law. Men feared God and the law because there was no way to satisfy the law apart from the death of the guilty. Jesus Christ came to be the Savior of men from the guilt, the bondage, and the fear of the law.

Speaking of the law's accusations against us, Paul writes that Jesus Christ blotted out the handwriting of the indictment against us. He "took it out of the way, nailing it to his cross; and having spoiled principalities and powers, he made a shew of them openly, triumphing over them in it" (Col. 2:14–15). By His death Christ satisfied the demands of the law so that we might be set free.

We were also in bondage to sin. We had no love for God, no desire to do the will of God. We loved sin, and we obeyed its pull. All that human nature produced was sin in the sight of God— totally unacceptable to Him. God saw that the heart of man was "only evil continually" (Gen. 6:5).

In Colossians 1:14, following his declaration that we have been delivered from the power of Satan, Paul declares of Christ, "In whom we have redemption through his blood, even the forgiveness of sins." The word "forgive" means to put away, to separate the sinner from his sins so that we bear them no longer. In

Colossians 2:13 Paul writes, "And you, being dead in your sins and the uncircumcision of your flesh, hath he quickened together with him, having forgiven you all trespasses." This forgiveness not only means that God has lifted the burden of sin, but it also means that God has taken us from the mastery of sin, so that we might serve a new master.

Christ also came to be Savior from the realm of death. There are two aspects of death as the penalty for sin. When God said to Adam, "In the day that thou eatest thereof thou shalt surely die" (Gen. 2:17), God was speaking primarily of spiritual death. Spiritual death is the separation of the soul from God. Had man not sinned, had he continued in his intimate fellowship with God, man would have lived forever. The seeds of corruption were not in his body at Creation, but the moment Adam disobeyed God spiritual death fell upon him. Adam was separated from God by a great gulf over which he could not cross. The result of spiritual death was physical death. It came as the penalty for Adam's separation from God.

The apostle Paul makes it clear that Christ came to save the world from bondage to death. Paul writes, "For the wages of sin is death; but the gift of God is eternal life through Jesus Christ our Lord." Eternal life is the life of God imparted to the one who trusts Christ as Savior.

How precious are our Lord's words given to us in John 10, where we see that Christ is the Savior from death. "And I give unto them eternal life; and they shall never perish, neither shall any man pluck them out of my hand. My Father, which gave them me, is greater than all; and no man is able to pluck them out of my Father's hand. I and my Father are one" (John 10:28–30). Jesus Christ came into the realm of spiritual death. He was separated from God, when He cried on the cross, "My God, my God, why hast thou forsaken me?" By that cry He is testifying that He left the realm of life and entered the realm of spiritual death that men might pass from death unto life through Him.

John also writes that Christ lifts man out of physical death into the newness of life.

> Verily, verily I say unto you, The hour is coming, and now is, when the dead shall hear the voice of the Son of God: and they that hear shall live. For as the Father hath life in himself; so hath he given to the Son to have life in himself; and hath given him authority to execute judgment also, because he is the Son of man. Marvel not at this: for the hour is coming, in the which all that are in the graves shall hear his voice, and shall come forth [the physically dead]; they that have done good, unto the resurrection of life, and they that have done evil, unto the resurrection of damnation (John 5:25–29).

The unsaved man lives with an uncontrollable fear of death because of the conviction in his heart that after death is the judgment. No man is prepared to stand alone before a holy and righteous Judge. But Jesus Christ is the Savior, not only from death, but also from the fear of death. For the child of God has the assurance given to us in 2 Corinthians 5:8, "To be absent from the body, [is] to be present with the Lord." There is no long journey, no dark valley, no time interval, we are immediately transformed out of this life into the presence of the Lord Jesus Christ. This hope is the result of God giving His Son to be our Savior.

Study Questions

1. What does the word *savior* mean?
2. What has Christ done to save us from bondage to Satan?
3. What has Christ done to save us from bondage to law?
4. What has Christ done to save us from bondage to sin?
5. What has Christ done to save us from bondage to death?

22

LOVE PERFECTED

1 John 4:16–21

THROUGH HIS ASSOCIATION WITH JESUS during His earthly ministry, John gave his heart to the Lord.

In chapters 3 and 4 of this epistle John has been appealing to the hearts of believers by emphasizing one command, "Love one another." As John concludes, he is speaking of the perfection of love. God, who has begun a process, is concerned with its conclusion. He wants to bring us to conformity to Jesus Christ. Therefore we read, "He that dwelleth in love dwelleth in God, and God in him" (v. 16).

The word *dwell* is one of John's favorites. He has used it throughout this epistle. It is variously translated to abide, to remain, or to dwell.

To dwell in God is to have one's spiritual roots so deeply implanted in Him that His life flows through the total person and manifests itself in our life. The plant sends roots into the soil, drawing moisture and nutrients that supply life. In the same way, when one is abiding in the love of God this love will permeate the person's personality so that he will live a different life before men. Men will see the love of God in him.

God is not saying that if we love Him as we ought then He dwells in us. He is saying that if we love one another, then the love of God is dwelling in us. When we are in right relationship to members of the family of God, we can be in right relationship to God Himself. John speaks of love made perfect in verse 17. God's intention when He gave His love to us was to make us perfect. Paul states in Romans 8:29 that it is God's plan that we might be conformed to the image of His Son. God wants to reproduce Jesus Christ in His children so that when a nonbeliever looks at the child of God, he will come to know the Father.

Paul is dealing with this same thought when he writes in Romans 13:8–10,

> For he that loveth another hath fulfilled the law. For this, Thou shalt not commit adultery, Thou shalt not kill, Thou shalt not steal, Thou shalt not bear false witness, Thou shalt not covet; and if there be any other commandment, it is briefly comprehended in this saying, namely, Thou shalt love thy neighbour as thyself. Love worketh no ill to his neighbour; therefore love is the fulfilling of the law.

In revealing the holiness of God, the law shows the life a man must live if he is to fellowship with a holy God. God wants to fulfill the righteousness of Christ in each of His children by reproducing Christ in each of them. God has given us His love so that we might be controlled in our relationships to one another.

The presence of this love in the child of God gives him boldness to approach the Father. Our love is made perfect "that we may have boldness in the day of judgment: because as he is, so are we in this world" (v. 17). This boldness is the freedom to come into the presence of God. This is the freedom Adam had before the fall. God and Adam enjoyed intimate fellowship in the garden, but he lost his freedom when he sinned. How can we who are sinners by nature and by choice be free to come into the presence of a holy God who condemns sin? It is because we have been made like Jesus.

In Jesus Christ we stand as men who are righteous in the sight of God. That glorious fact gives us boldness. We have freedom to come into the presence of God. That is why the writer to the Hebrews can say, "Let us therefore come boldly unto the throne of grace, that we may obtain mercy, and find grace to help in time of need" (4:16). We do not crawl into the presence of God; we come before Him with the full confidence that we have been accepted in Christ. We know that "there is therefore now no condemnation to them which are in Christ Jesus" (Rom. 8:1).

The one in whom love is perfected also lives without fear. "There is no fear in love; but perfect love casteth out fear" (v. 17). The word *fear* in the Word of God is used in two different senses. The first usage refers to reverence, or awe and respect. The child of God never loses his reverence for God, his sense of unworthiness as he approaches the glory of God. And it is right that we should fear God, but this is not what John is talking about when he says there is no fear in love.

John uses the word to denote dread or terror. When John speaks of "no fear" he means that Christ's love casts out our dread of God. It is respect for the Person that produces a godly awe, but it is sin that produces fear.

John has commanded us over and over again to love one another; to love God; to love the family of God. To safeguard against the misconception that we originate this love, John writes in verse 19, "We love him, because he first loved us." The love that perfects us and the love that gives us boldness and the love that removes fear does not originate with man, but it originates with God. Any affection that a man offers to God did not originate in his heart, because man hates God. But when God showers His love on us, that cold heart of stone is transformed so that it responds to the love of God.

In commanding us to "love one another," John is not saying that believers must generate this love in their own hearts. He is saying rather, that if they open their hearts to the love of God this love will produce love for God and love for the family of God. John could command us to love, but we could not do it. However,

God can flood the heart with His love so that we love.

John concludes in verses 20 and 21 by assuring us that the love of God will manifest itself in love for the brethren. "If a man say, I love God, and hateth his brother, he is a liar: for he that loveth not his brother whom he hath seen, how can he love God whom he hath not seen? And this commandment have we from him, That he who loveth God love his brother also."

The apostle Paul tells of his persuasion that "neither death, nor life, nor angels, nor principalities, nor powers, nor things present, nor things to come, nor height, nor depth, nor any other [creation], shall be able to separate us from the love of God, which is in Christ Jesus our Lord" (Rom 8:38–39). We cannot be separated from God, and that love is to so permeate our beings that it manifests itself not only in loving God but also in becoming a channel through which God loves others.

Study Questions

1. What does it mean to "dwell in God?"
2. How can a believer reveal God?
3. Relate love and boldness.
4. Explain how love casts out fear.
5. Why is love for a brother so necessary for a love for God?

23

OVERCOMING THE WORLD

1 John 5:1–5

MANY OF THE DECISIONS WE MAKE have a major effect on our life: the schools we attend, the person we marry, the profession we follow, the position we accept. But there is no decision with such wide-spread influence for time and eternity as the decision we make about Jesus Christ. John speaks of this decision and the new birth that results as he opens chapter 5. "Whosoever believeth that Jesus is the Christ is born of God. . . ."

The term *Christ* or *Messiah* embodies much biblical truth. It brings to our attention both the person and the work of the Lord Jesus Christ. According to the Old Testament, the One who came to be the Messiah would not only be the Son of David but He would also be the Son of God. During the course of His earthly life, Jesus Christ laid less claim to being Mary's son, and He placed more emphasis on being the Son of God. Man could not redeem man; only God could do that.

After offering Himself to Israel as the Messiah, Christ authenticated His person by the many miracles He performed. As the disciples saw the wonders and signs that came from His hands, they were led to the conviction that this One was the Son of God. They believed on Him (Matt. 16:16). Salvation depends on accepting the person of Jesus Christ, consenting to the biblical truth that

He is the Son of God. Faith itself does not save; it is a Person, the Savior, who saves.

The term *Messiah* also brings to our attention the work of Christ. God made it clear in the Old Testament that without the shedding of blood there is no remission of sin. The Messiah is described in Isaiah: "He was wounded for our transgressions, he was bruised for our iniquities: the chastisement of our peace was upon him; and with his stripes we are healed. All we like sheep have gone astray; we have turned every one to his own way; and the LORD hath laid on him the iniquity of us all" (Isa. 53:5–6). The Messiah must become their sin-bearer in death. One who comes to Christ not only trusts Him as a Person, but he also trusts His work at Calvary. There sinless blood was shed to provide a covering for the sins of the world, and we must trust in this work of Christ.

In verse 5 John says that whoever believes that Jesus is the Christ, or Messiah, is "born of God." John next presents three evidences of the new birth.

"Every one that loveth him that begat loveth him also that is begotten of him" (v. 5). This is the summary of what John has presented in chapters 3 and 4 so emphatically. God has commanded those who love Him to demonstrate this love by loving those whom He loves. Love for the brethren becomes the first evidence of the new birth.

Love cannot originate in the heart of a natural man because he is selfish and his love is directed inward. When one can go beyond the bounds of natural love and manifest the love of God, when one can love unselfishly, this is evidence of being born into the family of God.

After a worship service in Africa in which I had the privilege of taking part, one of the missionaries handed me a poem by an anonymous writer entitled "Perfect Love." In a simple and practical style these lines describe our love for fellow believers.

Slow to suspect,
> Quick to trust.
Slow to condemn,
> Quick to justify.
Slow to offend,
> Quick to defend.
Slow to expose,
> Quick to shield.
Slow to reprimand,
> Quick to forebear.
Slow to belittle,
> Quick to appreciate.
Slow to demand,
> Quick to give.
Slow to hinder,
> Quick to help.
Slow to provoke,
> Quick to conciliate.
Slow to resent,
> Quick to forgive.

In verses 2 and 3, John presents a second evidence of the new birth. "By this we know that we love the children of God, when we love God, and keep his commandments. For this is the love of God, that we keep his commandments: and his commandments are not grievous." The second proof of the new birth is obedience to the Word of God. The Lord said: "If a man love me, he will keep my words. . . . He that loveth me not keepeth not my sayings" (John 14:23–24). Or again in John 15:10, "If ye keep my commandments, ye shall abide in my love."

There in the upper room Jesus impressed on the disciples that God expected implicit obedience to His Word as an evidence of their love. Disobedience is essentially a sin against love. For one to profess to love God and refuse to obey His commandments is not a sign of affection, it is a sign of hatred. Hatred and disobedience are equated in the thinking of the apostle.

The Lord made this clear when He spoke to the Pharisees, who considered themselves to be the sons of God. He told the parable of the man and two sons. The father told the first son to go, and he consented, but he did not go. He told the second son to go, and he refused, but then went out and did what his father had commanded. The Lord asked the Pharisees which of the two was truly the son of his father. Unable to escape the logic of our Lord's presentation, they replied that the true son was the one who did what the father commanded. Doing the will of God, rather than merely discussing it, is a proof of sonship.

The last phrase in verse 3, "his commandments are not grievous," refers to our attitude toward the will of God and the Word of God. Many believers think that the will of God is something to be endured. They take up their cross and stumble along crushed by the will of God. But John says the will of God is not grievous. Submission to the will of God allows the grace of God to help us adapt to difficult curcumstances.

In verses 4 and 5 John gives a third evidence of the new birth: the one born again overcomes the world. "For whatsoever [or whosoever] is born of God overcometh the world: and this is the victory that overcometh the world, even our faith. Who is he that overcometh the world, but he that believeth that Jesus is the Son of God?"

Overcoming the world means that one manifests love of God and love of God's truth instead of the hatred displayed by the worldling.

John is not thinking here of the things that are in the world, things we so often characterize as being worldly. He is talking about the world's hatred of Jesus Christ. And the only way that one can rise above the attitude of the world, the only way one can rise above that basic sin nature with which he was born is to walk by faith.

Study Questions

1. Explain the term "the Christ" or "Messiah."
2. What two works are particularly emphasized in the biblical teaching about Messiah?
3. Explain the relationship of love and assurance.
4. Explain the relationship of obedience and assurance.
5. Explain the relationship of victory and assurance.

24

THE WITNESS OF THE SPIRIT

1 John 5:6–12

IN THE UPPER ROOM Christ promised the disciples that He would send the Holy Spirit, who would bear testimony to His works and to His person. "Howbeit when he, the Spirit of truth, is come, he will guide you into all truth: for he shall not speak of himself; but whatsoever he shall hear, that shall he speak: and he will shew you things to come. He shall glorify me . . ." (John 16:13–14).

In chapter 5 John presents several witnesses to Jesus Christ. In the sixth verse he says the Spirit bears witness to Jesus because the Spirit is truth. And again in verse 8, "And there are three that bear witness in earth, the Spirit, and the water, and the blood: and these three agree in one."

The Spirit's witness through water takes us back to Matthew 3, where John the Baptist presents a message to Israel, a people who had long been in darkness. "Repent ye; for the kingdom of heaven is at hand. . . . Prepare ye the way of the Lord, make his paths straight" (Matt. 3:2–3). Many confessed their sin and were baptized in the Jordan. John's baptism was based on repentance— confessing sin and turning to righteousness. The Spirit has had an agelong ministry of reproving and rebuking—convincing men that they are sinners in need of salvation. In the ritual of the people of Israel water signified cleansing; so John's baptism signified cleansing from sin. The ministry of the Spirit is first of all, then, to convince men that they are sinners and that they are in need of a Savior.

The Spirit bears testimony through blood that God has provided for man's need. The Old Testament is encapsulated in the Book of Hebrews: "Without shedding of blood is no remission" (Heb. 9:22). Water could not take away sin; only blood can do this. That is why Peter wrote,

> Forasmuch as ye know that ye were not redeemed with corruptible things, as silver and gold, from your vain conversation received by tradition from your fathers; but with the precious blood of Christ, as of a lamb without blemish and without spot: who verily was foreordained before the foundation of the world, but was manifest in these last times for you (1 Peter 1:18–20).

The Spirit convinces sinners that if they turn in faith to Jesus Christ and trust His blood, they will receive the gift of eternal life. Paul writes, "But after that the kindness and love of God our Saviour toward man appeared, not by works of righteousness which we have done, but according to his mercy he saved us, by the washing of regeneration, and renewing of the Holy Ghost; which he shed on us abundantly through Jesus Christ our Saviour" (Titus 3:4–6).

God the Father also witnesses to Jesus. John speaks of this in verse 9, "If we receive the witness of men, the witness of God is greater."

God authenticated the person of Jesus at His baptism: "This is my beloved Son, in whom I am well pleased" (Matt. 3:17). On the Mount of Transfiguration, Peter, James, and John heard this authentication a second time (Matt. 17:5). The witness of the Father coincides with that of the Spirit—Jesus is the sinless One and His sacrifice avails for sinners.

Finally, John records that there is a witness within the child of God.

> He that believeth on the Son of God hath the witness in
> himself: he that believeth not God hath made him a liar;
> because he believeth not the record that God gave of his Son.
> And this is the record, that God hath given to us eternal life,
> and this life is in his Son. He that hath the Son hath life; and
> he that hath not the Son of God hath not life (vv. 10–12).

The eternal God fellowships with us by sharing His life with us.
He invites us to share the security and the assurance that comes
from believing Him.

Study Questions

1. What is the Spirit's witness to Christ?
2. How does the Spirit use water to witness to Christ?
3. How does the Spirit use blood to witness to Christ?
4. What response to the Spirit's witness is required?
5. How is the Spirit's witness strengthened by the Father's
   witness?

25

ASSURANCE OF ETERNAL LIFE

1 John 5:13–15

IN 1 JOHN 5:13–15 the apostle gives us reasons why he has shared the witness of the Father and the Spirit to Jesus.

> These things have I written unto you that believe on the name of the Son of God; that ye may know that ye have eternal life, and that ye may believe on the name of the Son of God. And this is the confidence that we have in him, that, if we ask any thing according to his will, he heareth us: and if we know that he hear us, whatsoever we ask, we know that we have the petitions that we desired of him.

John wrote his Gospel to lead men to faith in the person of Jesus Christ, that through Him they might receive the gift of eternal life. To establish the validity of that gift John presented a number of Christ's miracles.

John's epistle gives us the witness of the Father and the Spirit to the person of Jesus Christ. The purpose of Gospel miracles and these witnesses in 1 John is the same—"that ye may believe on the name of the Son of God."

In verse 13 John tells of another reason for writing this epistle. "That ye may know that ye have eternal life." John wrote to assure us that as soon as we believe on Christ we enter into eternal life.

There are multitudes today who have accepted Christ as personal Savior but who would have difficulty answering the question, "Are you saved?" They might reply, "I hope so." "Do you have assurance of eternal life?" They might reply, "No. I don't believe any person has the right to say he has eternal life. We must wait until we stand in judgment; only then will we know if we have eternal life." What a tragedy that they do not rest in the promise of God that the one who receives Christ has eternal life the moment he believes. Failure to realize this has nothing to do with our eternal destiny, but it certainly affects our stay here on earth.

If one lives in fear and uncertainty, he cannot enter into the peace of God. What a comfort it is to know that the moment we accept Christ as personal Savior, God shares His eternal life with us, and we become his partner. God has nothing to give us in eternity that we do not possess this very moment other than the experience of glory itself.

When we look into verse 14, we find another reason John wrote. "This is the confidence that we have in him, that if we ask any thing according to his will, he heareth us." God is accessible. This is peculiar to Christianity. In other religions God is inaccessible.

This is clearly revealed in the contest between Elijah and the prophets of Baal (1 Kings 18). Four hundred fifty prophets implored Baal to demonstrate that he was God by consuming their sacrifice with fire. But they had no assurance that in uniting their voices they could gain the attention of their god, so they leaped on the altar to attract his attention. They even cut themselves as though the bullock on the altar was not enough. What a picture of men futilely trying to arouse an inaccessible god!

How blessed we are that God is accessible. Jesus has opened the way into heaven and bids us, "Come unto me, all ye that labour and are heavy laden, and I will give you rest" (Matt. 11:28). This is why the Lord Jesus could remind us that the heavenly Father who looks after the birds of the air and the grass of the field looks out for us (Matt. 6:26,30).

The writer to the Hebrews also speaks of this: "Let us hold fast our profession. For we have not an high priest which cannot be touched with the feelings of our infirmities; but was in all points tempted like as we are, yet without sin. Let us therefore come boldly unto the throne of grace, that we may obtain mercy, and find grace to help in time of need" (Heb. 4:14–16).

Between God and the sinner was a barrier that no man could penetrate. After His death Christ, as our priest, parted the veil so that we were given free access to the presence of God. The Lord Jesus as our representative stands in the presence of God. Since He walked among men, He knows all of the weaknesses and burdens to which we are heir.

In verse 15 John tells us, "If we know that he hear us, whatsoever we ask, we know that we have the petitions that we desired of him." John is assuring us that the God who hears will also answer prayer. God will respond to the cry of His child and will meet his need.

Prayer is an attitude of total dependence on God. Prayer is not pouring requests into the ear of God. God already knows the need. Prayer is consciously depending on God to meet our need in accordance with the promises of His Word. When the child of God depends on God, God's hand is moved.

In verse 14 John states, "If we ask any thing according to his will, he heareth us." Not every petition that the child of God presents to God is guaranteed fulfillment. The Lord had laid the foundation for this teaching in the upper room when He said, "Whatsoever ye shall ask in my name, that will I do" (John 14:13). And again, "If ye abide in me, and my words abide in you, ye shall ask what ye will, and it shall be done unto you" (15:7). When the child of God claims the promise of the Word of God as he prays to the Father, that prayer is certain to be answered. However, God gives no attention to what is prayed apart from the promises of His Word. For a prayer to be in accord with the will of God, it must be in harmony with the Word of God.

In daily life we accept the testimony of men. A word of assurance from a salesman concerning his product encourages us to buy. How much more we should accept the assurance from God the Father and God the Spirit as they authenticate the offer of the Son.

Study Questions

1. What was John's primary purpose in writing about the Spirit's witness?
2. What is a second result of receiving the Spirit's witness?
3. What is a third result of receiving the Spirit's witness?
4. How does the Spirit bring assurance?
5. What is the relationship of the Father's witness and that of the Spirit?

26

Sin unto death

1 John 5:16–17

SIN MAKES IT IMPOSSIBLE for a child of God to fellowship with his heavenly Father until it is confessed and he receives forgiveness. John has shown us in this epistle what fellowship involves and demands. In verses 15 and 16 we see God's great concern about our fellowship with Him.

John here deals with sin in God's child and God's response to this sin. God divides the sins of His children into two classifications: sin not unto death, and sin unto death. In verse 16 John says, "If any man see his brother sin a sin which is not unto death, he shall ask, and he shall give him life. . . ."

What is a believer to do when he sees a fellow believer sin? John says, "Let him ask." He is to petition God. He is not told to ask for forgiveness, because the prayer of one believer cannot accomplish forgiveness for another. This prayer can move the hand of God to discipline the guilty party so that he will confess his sin and be restored to fellowship with God.

John promises that God "shall give him life for them that sin not unto death." John is referring to the life of intimate fellowship that Jesus enjoyed with the Father while He was here among men. The Lord Jesus, who possesses the eternal life of God, had come into the world to demonstrate His life of fellowship with the Father so

that men might enter into this same fellowship. John is not referring to the gift of eternal life that will culminate our salvation. John
is saying that God will restore the erring believer to the intimacy of
fellowship that was marred by his sin.

In verse 16 John gives us a sober and, to many, unsettling word.
"There is a sin unto death." This is the second classification of
sin. Many people are confused about what John is teaching because they equate sin unto death with the unpardonable sin in
Matthew 12. However, the two are quite different.

After Jesus had cast the demon out of the blind and dumb man
and enabled him to see and to speak, the multitude said that only
God could perform such a miracle. They were acknowledging that
Jesus was who He professed to be—God's Son come into the
world to save sinners and to sit on David's throne.

The religious leaders became frenzied when they heard this
confession, and they ran among the people crying, "This fellow
doth not cast out devils, but by Beelzebub the prince of the devils"
(v. 24). They said Jesus was the son of Satan. The people therefore
faced these contrary interpretations.

Jesus had been offering Himself to the covenant nation Israel as
their Savior and as their king; He was calling on them to decide
about His person. This Word of Jesus was substantiated by the
miracles that the Holy Spirit produced through Him. The miracles
Christ did were not His own, they were the Father's. The Father
was testifying by the Spirit to the Word of the Son. There were two
witnesses to Jesus Christ—His own testimony and the testimony
of the Spirit through miracles.

If an individual accepted the testimony of Jesus, he did not need
the miracles. By faith he came to salvation. If a man rejected the
testimony of the Lord Jesus, he might still be brought to faith by
the testimony of the Spirit in miracles. But if he rejects the first
witness, the Word of Christ, and the second witness, the miracles
of the Spirit, there were no further witnesses that God provided to
lead men to faith in Christ.

So Jesus warned them:

All manner of sin and blasphemy shall be forgiven unto men: but the blasphemy against the Holy Ghost shall not be forgiven unto men. And whosoever speaketh a word against the Son of man, it shall be forgiven him: but whosoever speaketh against the Holy Ghost, it shall not be forgiven him, neither in this world [age], neither in the world to come" (vv. 31–32).

The Lord Jesus, then, is warning this generation that if they ignore His testimony and attribute miracles to the power of Satan, their fate is sealed, for God has no further witness to give them. They will be guilty of a sin that cannot be forgiven. That sin came to its consummation when the leaders in Israel said, "Crucify him. . . . We have no king but Caesar" (John 19:15). God judged Israel to be guilty of this sin when they crucified Jesus.

The Lord Jesus must be present before anyone can be guilty of the unpardonable sin. He must be ministering to the chosen people of Israel, offering Himself to them as their Savior and King. He must be performing miracles to prove His claim. Therefore, after the Resurrection this sin is no longer possible.

What, then, did John have in mind when he said, "There is a sin unto death"? First of all, we must determine what kind of death John is talking about here. Is this physical or spiritual death? There are many who understand John to mean that there is a sin that will lead to spiritual death—the loss of salvation. But such an interpretation is contrary to the consistent teaching of the Word of God concerning the sins of those who trust Christ as their personal Savior.

In Psalm 103:12 the psalmist says, "As far as the east is from the west, so far hath he removed our transgressions from us." In Isaiah 44:22 the prophet assures that God has "blotted out, as a thick cloud, all thy transgressions." Micah 7:19 states that God would cast sin into the depths of the sea, where no light can penetrate and where they can never be seen again. In Isaiah 38:17

God said He would cast our sins behind His back. That means He will literally put our sins between His shoulder blades and no one has yet seen what is between his shoulder blades. God is figuratively saying He will put our sins where they cannot be seen again. In Jeremiah 31:34 God says, "I will remember their sin no more." By an act of His will God can dismiss from His memory every sin that has been put under the blood of Christ. In Romans 8:1 Paul says, "There is therefore now no condemnation [judgment] to them which are in Christ Jesus." John 5:24 states: "He that heareth my word, and believeth on him that sent me, hath everlasting life, and shall not come into condemnation [judgment]; but is passed from death unto life."

Those are only a few of the many verses telling us that when our sins are covered by the blood of Christ they are dismissed from God's memory. The record is made clean, and there is no indictment lodged against us. If the phrase "There is a sin unto death" meant that the guilty would lose their salvation, John would be denying the clear and consistent testimony of the Word of God. John cannot be writing about spiritual death. He is saying that there is such a thing as sin that ends in physical death.

Not all sin, John has told us in verse 16 and again in 17, ends in physical death. But some sin may result in physical death. To understand this we must understand something of the discipline of God. We are told in Hebrews 12 that just as our human fathers discipline us, so God our heavenly Father disciplines us. The human father, because of his compassion for his child, disciplines gently at first. He increases the discipline according to need until the desired end is accomplished.

This is God's method of discipline. This is borne out graphically in Hosea 5, where the prophet is speaking of the sin of Israel. He is warning them that because of their infidelity to God, God must discipline them. He says in verse 12, "Therefore will I be unto Ephraim as a moth." A moth destroys slowly. But in verse 14 we read, "I will be unto Ephraim as a lion." The lion strikes with force and destroys. If the nation would heed the prophet's warning and turn to God, God's discipline would be light. But if they ignore the warnings, God's discipline would become heavier and heavier until Assyria, like a ravaging lion, would carry them away into captivity.

We find the same concept in Hebrews 12:5–6, "Ye have forgotten the exhortation which speaketh unto you as unto children, My son, despise not thou the chastening of the Lord, nor faint when thou are rebuked of him, for whom the Lord loveth he chasteneth, and scourgeth every son whom he receiveth." Three words here signify a progression in God's discipline: "chastening"; "rebuke"; and "scourging." The final discipline God imposes on His child is a premature physical death, by which the individual who resisted restoration to fellowship with God is taken into the fellowship God has prepared for His children.

God does not punish His children for their sins. Thank God for that! Punishment is retribution for wrong. Jesus bore the punishment for the believer's sin on the cross. God's purpose in discipline is stated twice in Hebrews 12. We read in verse 10, "He chastens for our profit, that we might be partakers [fellowshipers] of His holiness." God disciplines to restore us after broken fellowship. Again in verse 11, "No chastening for the present seemeth to be joyous, but grievous: nevertheless afterward it yieldeth the peaceable fruit of righteousness." Righteousness is the product of fellowship.

We have a number of illustrations in Scripture of sin unto death. In Leviticus 10, Nadab and Abihu, because of their rebellion, were consumed with fire. In Numbers 16, Korah, his sons, and two hundred fifty priests were swallowed up into the earth. In Acts, Ananias and Sapphira professed to give themselves totally to God and to the saints but God took their lives because their profession was a lie.

The purpose of these deaths was twofold: first, to bring the impenitent one to fullness of fellowship with God; second, to be a lesson to the saints of the peril of unconfessed sin. God does not regard broken fellowship lightly. To live with unconfessed sin is to invite discipline.

Many, no doubt, are asking, "If there is a sin unto death, please tell me quickly what it is so that I can avoid it at any cost." It should be said that this text should read, "There is such a thing as sin unto death." John did not have a specific sin in mind. Any sin not confessed could result in a premature physical death for the child of God.

John says in verse 16, "I do not say that he shall pray for it." The word translated "pray" is a different word from the word translated "ask" earlier in this verse. You will get the force of what John is saying if we read the latter part of verse 16 this way: "There is such a thing as sin unto death. I do not say that he shall make inquiry about it." If a believer is near death but there is no evidence of unconfessed sin, we are not to ask, "What did he do to deserve this?" This presupposes that all sickness is the discipline of God for sin, but this is not biblical. We do not inquire about such matters, even if the individual dies. That is a matter between God and that individual.

John writes that God is so concerned about our fellowship with Him that He will use whatever means are necessary to restore us to fellowship. If His discipline is resisted, God's hand will become heavier and heavier until we are brought to confession. Should we fail to confess, God might remove us by physical death to bring us into that fellowship for which we were born again.

Study Questions
  1. What does sin do to a believer's fellowship?
  2. What death is in view in the sin unto death?
  3. How do you know this death is not spiritual death?
  4. How does a believer avoid God's discipline when he sins?
  5. What are God's steps in disciplining His child?

LYING IN THE LAP OF WICKEDNESS

1 John 5:18–21

RELIGION WAS DESIGNED to make worldly people otherworldly. James states, "Pure religion and undefiled before God and the Father is this, To visit the fatherless and widows in their affliction, and to keep himself unspotted from the world" (1:27). There are two evidences of the validity of a man's faith: first, it produces a selfless love; second, it keeps a man unspotted from the world.

John develops the same truths in 1 John 5:18–21. The first manifestation of the life of Christ is that a man will love unselfishly. The second, a man's conduct will be so transformed that his life will be patterned after another world.

When John says, "We know that whosoever is born of God sinneth not," he is not teaching that it is impossible for a born-again believer to sin. This would be contrary to the teaching of the Word of God, for there we have a record of saints who, although they possessed eternal life, did commit sin. John is instead emphasizing that the one who has been born of God has been given a new nature. The nature of God is imparted to the child of God and is incapable of committing sin.

In 2 Peter 1:4 we read that God has "given to us exceeding great and precious promises: that by these ye might be partakers of the divine nature, having escaped the corruption that is in the world through lust." Peter sees the world as a place of corruption. The believer has been lifted out of that corruption. God, by a new birth, has imparted His own nature to him. God cannot sin. When God gives His nature to His child, that nature cannot sin.

While the child of God may operate at times by the old nature, it is no longer necessary for him to do so. The child of God sins only by refusing to permit the new nature to operate within him. Once it was necessary for us to live under the control of sin because we possessed only a fallen sin nature, but now we do this at the risk of divine discipline.

John explains why it is not necessary for the one born of God to live under the control of the old sin nature. He says in verse 18, "He that is begotten of God keepeth himself, and that wicked one toucheth him not." The word "keepeth" suggests setting a guard. The child of God who lives by the new nature sets a constant guard over his thoughts, words, actions, and his patterns of life to see that they are not conforming to the world's dictates.

The Word of God charges the believer with responsibility for his conduct. It is not possible for us to excuse our sin by saying, "Satan made me do it." Satan may have been the tempter, but we are no longer obligated to submit to his enticements. Neither does the child of God have the right to say, "Everybody is doing it; I only conformed to the standards of the world in which I live." For we have been lifted out of the world by the new birth. If a child of God patterns his conduct according to the world, he denies the Spirit of God in him.

John describes graphically the state of the world. "The whole world lieth in wickedness" (v. 19). Or, "The whole world is being cradled in the arms of the wicked one." The worldling, like a baby, is being cradled by the evil one. He is also being fed by the evil one; so he will reproduce the devil's wickedness.

The Word of God has a great deal to say about "the world"— the organized system under the control of Satan.

In John 12:31 Satan is called "the prince of this world." He is the one in control, before whom all his subjects bow in submission. In 1 Corinthians 1:21, Paul says, "The world by wisdom knew not God." It is ignorant of the living God because it knows only Satan. Peter writes of believers in 2 Peter 2:20: "They have escaped the pollutions of the world." The world defiles everything that touches it. In 2 Peter 1:4 the apostle also spoke of "the corruption that is in the world." The world breeds a pervasive kind of evil. The world, then, is the means by which Satan accomplishes his purpose of dethroning God and enthroning himself.

What is our safeguard against the world? "We know that the Son of God is come, and hath given us an understanding" (v. 20). We understand Satan's purpose and how he operates. The child of God puts himself on guard against being run in the mold of the world or "conformed," as Paul says in Romans 12:2.

Jesus was surrounded by the system of Satan, but He kept Himself from the world. His goals were never the goals that Satan works out through the worldling. His pattern of life was not the pattern of one who draws his strength from Satan. The things He held Himself responsible for were not what the world tells a man he ought to be doing. If we would enter into the fullness of life and experience the fullness of joy, we must be like the Lord Jesus.

John gives a concluding enjoinder. "Little children, keep yourselves from idols." What John had in mind is illustrated in the Old Testament. At the conclusion of forty years of wilderness wanderings, Israel was ready to enter into the land of promise. God gave a command to the children of Israel through Moses.

> And the LORD spake unto Moses in the plains of Moab by Jordan near Jericho, saying, Speak unto the children of Israel, and say unto them, When ye are passed over Jordan into the land of Canaan; Then ye shall drive out all the inhabitants of the land from before you, and destroy all their pictures, and destroy all their molten images, and quite pluck down all their high places [places of worship]: and ye shall dispossess the inhabitants of the land, and dwell therein: for I have given you the land to possess it (Num. 33:50–53).

When the children of Israel came into the land, they were to remain disassociated from the idolatry of the people and from the false gods. As a people set apart, they were to destroy every idol and the high places devoted to their worship. Every remnant of idolatry was to be put out of the land.

God knew that if they removed the idols but left the idolaters, Israel would soon be corrupted. Therefore God said they were also to drive out all the inhabitants of the land. Why? Because idolatry will corrupt godliness, as God warned Israel: "But if ye will not drive out the inhabitants of the land from before you; then it shall come to pass, that those which ye let remain of them shall be pricks in your eyes, and thorns in your sides, and shall vex you in the land wherein ye dwell" (Num. 33:55).

This is what John had in mind when he said to his children, "Keep yourselves from idols." There cannot be a marriage between the believer and the world. The believer cannot conform to the world and maintain the intimate life of fellowship with the Father. Fellowship with the Father demands complete separation from all that is in the world.

We were born into this world, but we were born again out of the world. We live in the midst of the world, but we need not be corrupted by the world. The child of God is held responsible to set a guard on his life so that the corruption of the world does not touch him. Only as we live the life of heaven in the midst of the world can we enjoy fellowship with the Father.

Study Questions

  1. Can a believer sin?
  2. What does John mean when he says "whosoever is born of God sinneth not"?
  3. What is John's instruction for preventing sin in a believer's life?
  4. What is the world's relationship to Satan?
  5. What is a believer's relationship to the world?